THE TEST YOURSELF BOOK

By Harry E. Gunn with Violet C. Gunn

Chicago Review Press, 820 N. Franklin, Chicago 60610

Copyright 1980 by Harry E. Gunn
All rights reserved
Printed in the United States of America
First edition
First printing
Published by Chicago Review Press, Chicago
ISBN 0-914090-96-8
Library of Congress Catalog Number 80-66752

**To all of those people who
love doing things together**

Acknowledgements

This book could not have been created without extensive help from a number of very skilled people. Chief among them was Mrs. Jacie Saunders, publisher of Calumet Index, Inc. Jacie's creativity and organizational abilities were particularly helpful, as was her artistic ability.

Dr. Robert Nyquist, a prominent Hinsdale, Illinois, psychiatrist, provided help in the area of clinical evaluations. Ms. Rose Fonct, M.S.N., also from Hinsdale, is a specialist in psychiatric nursing and has a further specialty in sexual dysfunction. With her expert training she was able to make very significant contributions to this book.

There were many others who provided great help in the development of this book, but they are too numerous to mention. We do, therefore, wish to thank them as a group.

About the Authors

Harry E. Gunn earned his doctoral degree in clinical psychology from Loyola University of Chicago and has applied his knowledge of psychology in widely different areas. For more than ten years he worked for the Illinois Department of Mental Health and during that tenure served as a consultant for an Office of Economic Opportunity project. Dr. Gunn was a consultant to a seven-school grade school district and was instrumental in establishing a testing program to identify gifted youngsters. Dr. Gunn also has worked with industrial firms to test executive applicants and to conduct sensitivity programs with higher echelon executives. He has had more than ten years of teaching experience and has supervised the testing procedures of other psychologists. In addition, Dr. Gunn has conducted psychological research, and has been a therapist. He has, along with his wife, taught sex education classes for preteenagers.

Most germane to the Test Yourself Book has been Dr. Gunn's work with psychological tests. For the past fifteen years he has functioned primarily as a clinical diagnostician. In this role, Dr. Gunn daily uses psychological tests to evaluate personality, both in business and in a clinical setting. Since 1977 he has worked with Personnel Security Corporation of Oak Brook, Illinois, where he evaluates sophisticated test data for prospective police and fire fighter candidates ranging over three states. Dr. Gunn sees approximately one thousand persons yearly for some sort of test evaluation, and he estimates that he has evaluated more than ten thousand persons during the last fifteen years.

Dr. Gunn is the author of a psychological study using test data, and has published a prior book, **Manipulation by Guilt,** that has recently appeared in France.

Violet C. Gunn has a background in art, psychology and business. She studied art at the Chicago Art Institute and the American Academy of Art in Chicago. Her active interest in psychology led her to participate with her husband in teaching sex education and in counseling teenagers and older couples.

Mrs. Gunn's knowledge of art has combined with her interest in psychology in the development of this book. She has contributed many hours of research to its creation.

CONTENTS

Introduction ix

1. Personality Trait Tests 1
   1. The Assertive Test
   2. A Test of Emotional Awareness
   3. The Conscience Test
   4. The Manipulation Test
   5. The Personal Equation Test

2. Tests of Marital Adjustment 29
   1. A Test of Marital Adjustment
   2. A Test of Desired Changes
   3. How Well Do You Know Your Mate?
   4. The Affairs Test—For Women Only
   5. The Affairs Test—For Men Only

3. Intelligence Tests 61
   1. The Vocabulary Test
   2. A Test of Abstract Intelligence
   3. The Proverb Test
   4. The Creative Intelligence Test

4. Personality Tests 75
   1. Description Personality Tests
   2. Sleep Test
   3. Measurement of Personality Adjustment
   4. The Color Test
   5. The Inkblot Test
   6. Handwriting Analysis

5. Tests of Sexual Interests, Knowledge and Preferences   129
1. A Test of Sexual Knowledge
2. A Pictorial Ranking of Women
3. A Pictorial Ranking of Men
4. A Woman's Test of Sexual Attraction
5. A Man's Test of Sexual Attraction

6. Preference Tests   157
1. Individual Scale of Values
2. Preferred Activities
3. A Test of Sexual Attitudes

7. Memory Tests   177
1. Memory for Digits
2. Memory for Objects
3. Memory for Designs

Introduction

Ever wonder what your IQ is, how knowledgeable you are about sex, how well adjusted you are, or how good your marriage is? Most of us ponder these questions but we never have a chance to find the answers.

Here is a book that will provide such answers—within the security, privacy and comfort of your own living room. The book contains dozens of tests that cover such areas as sexual adjustment, sexual preference, knowledge about sexual behavior, intellectual ability, word skills and knowledge. It has tests that will help you measure how well you communicate with people, your abstract ability, your problem solving ability, the power of your memory, and your facility to handle logic. Many tests also are provided for measuring personality traits, these ranging from interests to temperament to degrees of emotional maladjustment. A variety of tests is provided so that in some cases one looks at ink blots or shaded nudes, while other tests require only a yes or no answer. The tests easily can be self-scored—and besides being helpful, they provide hours of fun. There may be a great temptation to dive right into a book like this and begin the self-analysis. However, before the exploration begins, we would like everyone to read this chapter carefully. It should make the book more enjoyable, and there are some important words of caution that need to be noted.

The administration and interpretation of one form or another of personality tests has become a multimillion dollar industry in the United States and is increasing rapidly world wide. When a student applies to a college or university he or she usually is given some form of an educational test. Many other schools, including high schools, use academic tests to determine a student's learning aptitude. Increasingly, applicants are given a variety of tests when they apply for employment. It now is common knowledge that the military used tests extensively during World War II to pinpoint the talents of millions of men so they could be most effectively used to further the country's war effort.

Psychological tests also have been widely used to assess emotional make-up. During wartime, such tests screened out those draftees whose emotional make-up would not be suited to military life. Psychological tests also have been used to select individuals who have strong leadership ability, and to eliminate those who might be unable to function in highly stressful vocations, such as, for example, law enforcement.

Recently, psychological testing has come into its own in the clinical arena. Such testing is now generally used to evaluate those accused of antisocial acts—to determine their suitability for trial. Psychological testing also is used in the less dramatic (but highly important) context of determining sources of marital conflict. For example, Dr. Gunn has used psychological tests in order to find why couples fight over child-rearing practices. On a number of such occasions it was found that one parent was overly strict while the other was excessively lenient. Quite understandably, the children were very confused!

In clinical practice, psychological tests, psychiatric evaluation and the social worker's case history are combined to provide a more complete picture of the individual's personality. Properly used, clinical test data can give an objective and rapid assessment of how an individual functions. As people find out more about themselves they can more quickly locate better methods of dealing with their conflicts. We all have some conflicts; what is most important is the manner in which we deal with them. Knowledge can be power if we know how to use it, and self-knowledge can help people develop their psychological powers.

This book contains a large number of tests that cover many different aspects of personality. The reader should find clues about his or her intelligence, problem-solving ability, memory, personal adjustment, sexual knowledge, interests, personal preferences, and means of handling anger, to name only a few. This added knowledge should provide better self-evaluation and help strengthen marital relationships. In fact, all human relationships should improve with greater self-awareness. In addition, the test results, when shared with others, should help the reader better understand the needs of those close to him or her.

A Word of Caution . . .

Most people enjoy taking tests because they are curious to know something about themselves. Unfortunately, sometimes we find out things about ourselves that we don't like. For example, we hope to find that we are extremely intelligent, and perhaps the tests don't show us in that light. In that eventuality, the best of us are likely to suffer some ego shock.

The same kind of experience may take place when a couple compares test results. A husband may not like something that he discovers about his wife, for example. He may become critical of her and she angry at his criticism.

It is not the purpose of this book to be unpleasant or disruptive, but if the results of one test or another should disappoint you, please remember: NO TEST IS PERFECT!! Every test includes some degree of error. Generally, the error increases when the test is group-administered and decreases when it is administered one-to-one. Likewise, error increases when you take the test yourself and decreases when you are tested by a trained professional.

When a clinical psychologist tests a patient, he knows how to establish rapport and handle the patient's anxiety so as to maximize a test performance. Furthermore, the psychologist has administered many such tests and has read the results of many thousands more. He has a wide sampling of behavior against which to measure and interpret an individual's performance. It goes without saying that testing in the psychologist's office is much more likely to be accurate than testing in your own living room.

So if you feel uncomfortable with any of your test results, be sure to consider the possibility of error. If you continue to feel concern about yourself, the best approach is to seek direct help from a trained professional.

How These Tests Were Constructed
A test can be defined as "a sample of behavior." That sample, in order to be useful, must be representative of a larger grouping of behavior. For example, the ability to define words would be insignificant if it did not tell us something about general learning ability.

In order for a test score to be useful it must be able to predict a larger sample of behavior. A relationship must exist between a score and a performance, and that relationship is called a "correlation." A correlation is simply a means of expressing the degree of relationship between two variables. We all recognize that there is a high correlation between success in basketball and height. Most good basketball players are very tall. On the other hand, there is no correlation between foot size and learning ability.

If any test is to be useful (or valid) it must produce a score that bears a relationship to some performance. If a high score on an intelligence test, for example, correlates highly with school grades, it is a good test. If a high IQ score does not correlate with learning ability in school (or somewhere else), then that IQ test is useless.

Each of the tests presented in this book was created from the experiences of the authors. As each test was created, it was administered to groups of people. Data then was collected about those taking the various tests. This data consisted of other test scores, social history, school performance, and in some cases even ratings made by psychologists and psychiatrists. In every case, at least one hundred persons were used in the test standardization, and in some cases as many as two hundred fifty persons. Some tests were given by various experts, such as a sexual dysfunction therapist or a group counselor. No claim is made that the tests were found to be perfect, but it is clear from the results obtained that they did very well.

How To Take These Tests
Our first suggestion is that those taking the tests refrain from marking answers in the book. Mark your answers on separate sheets of paper and you will be able to use the book over and over again.

Secondly, you may derive greater enjoyment with these tests if you take them with that special person in your life. That would not be so true with the ability tests (as, for example, the intelligence tests), but it should be the case for the personality and interest tests.

Graphic representation is afforded for some of the test results. These graphs are easy to construct. For example, supposing on a test you earn the following scores after each trait:

xii

>   honesty   10
>   aggressiveness   8
>   introversion   6
>   impulsiveness   3
>   patience   9

Then your bar graph would look like this:

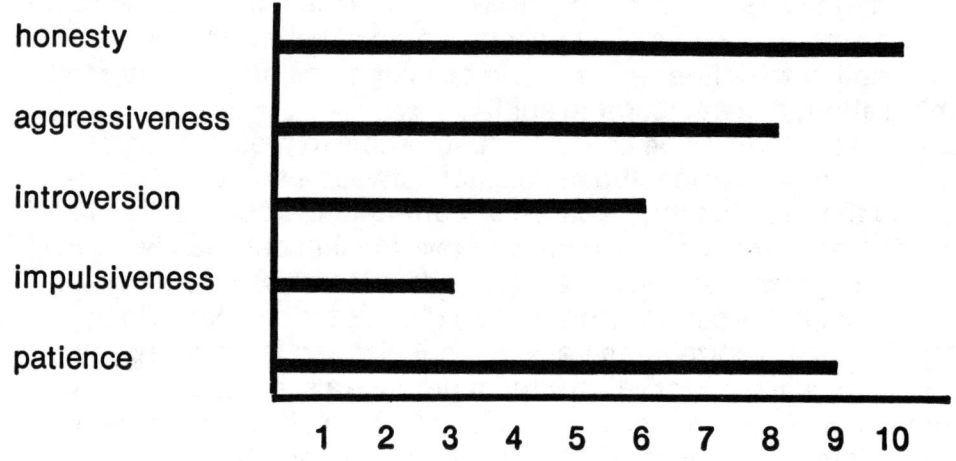

With a line graph the same scores would look like this:

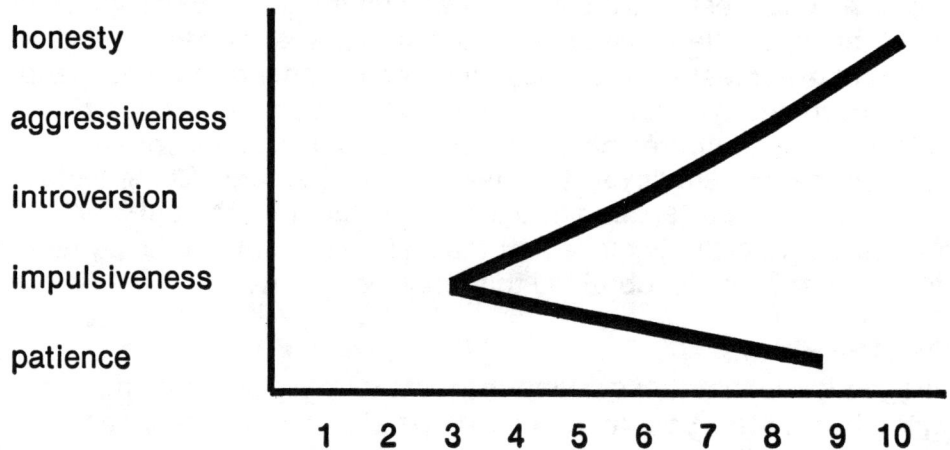

These two types of graphs should allow you easily to assess your profile. They are easy to construct.

One Final Word . . .
As you tackle these tests, you should increase your self-knowledge but, above all, please have fun. That's what it is all about.

1. Personality Trait Tests

1. The Assertive Test
2. A Test of Emotional Awareness
3. The Conscience Test
4. The Manipulation Test
5. The Personal Equation Test

A personality trait is some particular aspect of one's overall personality. A trait test is more specific than a personality test in as much as one's personality is composed of many, many traits.

The traits that we have selected for evaluation are important and the results should prove interesting. However, as you take these and the other tests try not to be overly critical of yourself. Always remember that no one is perfect and neither is any one test.

The Assertive Test

Introduction: Do others frequently take advantage of you? Do you shy away from conflict with others? Would you rather fight than switch? These are very important questions that need to be answered in order to evaluate your style of social interaction. From time to time each of us must deal with the hostility of others. In these situations, do we handle ourselves in keeping with our general ideals or do we react in kind and make the situation worse for ourselves? This test will help you determine how to deal with the aggressiveness of others, and it will allow you to consider modifying the way in which you interact with others.

Directions: For each of the following questions select the answer that you feel would best describe your behavior in a given situation. Then check the answers provided at the conclusion of the test.

1. Suppose one of your closest friends did something which affected you and you did not like it. What would you do?

a. Probably not say anything.
b. Try to talk it out with your friend.
c. Talk out the resultant anger with someone else.
d. Probably blow up.

2. You make a purchase and when you get it home discover a few parts are missing. The missing parts are not crucial but are useful. You likely would:

a. Immediately go back to the store and vent your anger.
b. Not do anything.
c. Call the manager and see what he is willing to do.
d. Never go back there again.

3. A sales clerk insults your style of dress, saying it is outdated. You would:

a. Laugh it off.
b. Tell the clerk you did not ask for an opinion.
c. Become angry and warn this uninvited critic not to do it again.
d. Leave the store.

4. At a bar a drunk insults you. You would:

a. Hit him (or slap him) if he refuses an apology.
b. Move to another spot.
c. Ignore him.
d. Tell the bartender to restore order.

5. Your child talks back to you. You are likely to:

a. Send the child to his or her room.
b. Talk to the child about handling anger.
c. Hit him or her.
d. Not say anything at the time.

6. Someone interrupts your conversation. You would:

a. Seethe on the inside but not comment on the interruption.
b. Withdraw from the conversation.
c. With mild humor point out what happened.
d. Angrily tell the person off.

7. Your senator sponsors a bill (law) that you dislike. You would:

a. Angrily call him.
b. Do nothing.
c. Talk against him.
d. Write him a letter explaining your opposition.

8. A policeman wrongly accuses you of an illegal turn. You are likely to:

a. Say nothing because you might make him angry.
b. Argue with him.
c. Refuse to support police charities from then on.
d. Blow your top regardless of what he does.

9. At a movie theater you leave for a drink. When you return, someone has taken your seat. You would:

a. Loudly demand that the interloper leave.
b. Quietly find another seat.
c. Tell that person that he or she has your seat.
d. Stand there until he or she moves.

10. A waitress spills a drink on you. You would:

a. Demand that the manager come out and look at the damage.
b. Tell her that it just isn't your day.
c. Refuse to speak to her.
d. Tell her that you wish to have the cleaning bill paid.

11. You order a steak cooked medium and it arrives well done. You would:

a. Eat it but refuse to leave a tip and never return.
b. Ask to see the manager so that it never will happen again.
c. Tell the waiter that you are sorry but that he will have to replace the steak.
d. Eat the steak and not make a fuss.

12. Someone at a party makes a statement about abortion, a position that is directly opposite yours. You probably would:

a. Tell that person that he or she is talking rubbish.
b. Keep your views to yourself.
c. Refuse to support that person by your silence.
d. Make an unemotional attempt to offer your opinion.

13. You are with three other people. They wish to see a movie you already have seen. You would:

a. Go along but refuse to laugh.
b. Tell them you have seen it and try to persuade the group to select another movie.
c. Go along and try to enjoy it.
d. Tell them you refuse to go.

14. Someone blows smoke in your face. You find that objectionable, particularly since you don't smoke yourself. You would:

a. Grin and bear it.
b. Silently leave.
c. Tell the smoke-blower that he or she is very rude.
d. Tell him or her that smoke disturbs you.

15. Your boss publicly berates something you have done. You would:

a. Ask your boss to discuss what he or she objects to.
b. Become angry and leave.
c. Become angry and fight back.
d. Lose your incentive to do good work.

16. Someone steals your parking place. You might well:

a. Wait until that person leaves and then scratch the paint on the offending car.
b. Explain that you were waiting for that spot.
c. Go find another spot.
d. Leave and go home.

17. Someone insults your spouse. You would:

a. Say that you don't care for such comments.
b. Ignore the person.
c. Make a nasty remark to that person's spouse.
d. Laugh it off.

18. A high-pressure salesman comes to your door. You would:

a. Slam the door in his face.
b. Tell him you aren't interested.
c. Let him make his salespitch and then not purchase from him.
d. Discuss his product.

19. Another parent tells you that his child is smarter than yours. You probably would:

a. Discuss it with him.
b. Walk away.
c. Tell him that you are pleased with your child.
d. Tell him that you aren't interested in what he is saying.

20. You see a friend drinking too much at a party. You probably would:

a. Inform your friend that you hate that kind of behavior.
b. Try to talk about this over-imbibing to see if something is bothering your friend.
c. Look the other way.
d. Accept this behavior and joke with your friend about it.

Scoring: There are four primary approaches to expressing aggressiveness or assertiveness. One of these is overt aggression, in which quick direct anger is expressed toward some person or object. A second is passive aggression, in which anger is expressed very indirectly, such as by withholding something of oneself from another person. A third would involve verbal assertiveness wherein an attempt is made to solve the problem (or conflict) by communication. Finally, there is accommodation or withdrawal, and this involves turning the anger inward.

Few people use one technique at all times, simply because life is too complex to resort to any one approach. Consequently it is best to construct your own profile to see which approaches you emphasize. This easily is done by checking those answers in the scoring key that you have selected. You then can construct your profile by counting the number of times you have used each approach and drawing a line on the graph to represent your number of choices. You are likely to find that one approach predominates. You then can raise the question as to whether you wish to change your approach to more adequately reach your goals. Or you may decide to stick with that which has worked. In any event, awareness of how you respond should provide flexibility.

The Assertive Test Key

	Overt Agression	Passive Agressive	Verbal Assertiveness	Accommodation or Withdrawal
1.	D	C	B	C
2.	A	D	C	B
3.	C	A	B	D
4.	A	C	D	B
5.	C	D	B	A
6.	D	A	C	B
7.	A	C	D	B
8.	D	C	B	A
9.	A	D	C	B
10.	A	B	D	C
11.	B	A	C	D
12.	A	C	D	B
13.	D	A	B	C
14.	C	A	D	B
15.	C	D	A	B
16.	A	C	B	D
17.	C	D	A	B
18.	B	C	D	A
19.	D	A	C	B
20.	A	D	B	C

Assertive Profile

Overt Aggression

Passive Aggressive

Verbal Assertiveness

Accommodation or Withdrawal

4	8	12	16	20

Frequency of Selection

A Test of Emotional Awareness

Introduction: Have you ever hurt the feelings of someone and wondered how it happened? For example, maybe you asked someone if he or she felt well and, because of your question, that person assumed that he or she must look unhealthy. Have you often been confused by the behavior of others? Do you feel that social interaction is enhanced by an understanding of the people involved and their motives?

Most of us would answer "yes" to these questions. The better we are able to read others, the more skilled we can become in relating to them. This test will help you evaluate your skills in understanding others and will identify strong and weak areas.

Directions: People have a way of not saying what they really mean. All of us have some tendency to cover up our deeper feelings. However, often we can tell by another person's behavior what underlying motives are involved. This test evaluates the reader's skill at determining what is taking place. In each of the 21 situations that follow, a small behavioral sample is provided. Write out a few words for each situation, "reading" the underlying message, and then check your interpretation with those that are provided in the section called **Analysis of Behavior For Scoring Answers.**

1. A person yawns while you are talking to him or her.

2. You are talking to someone at a party; a third party interrupts you.

3. Someone listens to you for a moment, then asks you to expand upon something you have said.

4. Another person says, "I did a really good job, didn't I?"

5. Someone talks to you about personal problems and then becomes angry at you.

6. At a party a wife says to her husband, "Gee, that girl really looks good in that dress, doesn't she?"

7. An executive says, "Oh well, athletes don't live very long, anyway."

8. You do something for a guilt-ridden person. That person thanks you and then, shortly thereafter, becomes angry.

9. You compliment someone and that person argues with you.

10. A woman says, "Men don't seek the affection that women do."

11. A man says, "Well, at least no woman can run with a football like O.J. Simpson."

12. A man who lost his job to a younger man says, "I don't really care. I will probably find something better."

13. A man says, "No woman is ever going to hurt me."

14. A person says, "It sure makes me mad the way everyone depends upon me for everything."

15. Another comment: "I don't think it's fun to go to a party where I don't know many of the people."

16. The comment is made, "No one in this world is better than I am!"

17. A person at a party says, "I think it is absolutely disgusting the way that person over there shows off!"

18. The statement is made: "I am not angry when people hurt me, for I know that they do not know any better."

19. Another person says, "Nothing really bothers me—I am well controlled and don't allow my emotions to rule me."

20. Another quotation: "I have an overpowering need to help people and I am disturbed when they won't let me. I often feel that no one can do for them what I can do."

21. One final quotation: "You are really smart. Can you tell me how to do this problem?"

Analysis of Behavior For Scoring Answers

1. The yawning person is showing either a lack of sleep, boredom and/or passive-aggressive hostility—saying in effect that he or she is not interested in the conversation.

2. The third person needs attention and demands it by interrupting. Such a person has little awareness of others.

3. Unlike the interrupter in the previous example, this person is a good listener and wishes to communicate. People enjoy individuals such as this.

4. This person simply is asking for support. Since everyone needs support and attention at some time, we can't say that insecurity is revealed.

5. This is the very difficult situation faced by psychologists and psychiatrists. In talking, some persons reveal some of their problems to *themselves.* This then may make them angry and they may well take it out on the listener, showing that listening may be dangerous.

6. A hard one to analyze without more information. If the wife is very secure, she is just paying a nice compliment. If she feels some insecurity, she wants her husband to tell her she looks nice, too. If the latter is the case, her husband better do so or she is likely to go out and buy more clothes.

7. An untrue statement that undoubtedly reveals envy.

8. The guilt-ridden person feels worthless and more guilt-ridden with praise. This guilt may cause anger which results in punishment to you. This person, sure of self-worthlessness, won't trust others.

9. When persons argue after receiving a compliment, they either want more compliments or else they are too insecure to accept praise.

10. In all probability, what she means is that *she* doesn't get all of the attention that *she* wants.

11. His male ego has been punctured and so this man falls back upon identification with a strong, skilled and successful man.

12. Here is a rationalization to protect the hurt ego.

13. If this statement is true, then the person has guarded his feelings to the extent that he has become isolated.

14. Persons who make this statement really need dependency or they

wouldn't allow it to happen. This statement attests to the fact that one may hate something that he or she needs.

15. Shy, insecure persons are afraid of new experiences.

16. Persons who make such a remark are trying to reassure themselves and are covering up their massive insecurity.

17. The speaker here resents others who are able to corner the attention that he or she would like. Otherwise the "disgust" wouldn't be necessary.

18. Persons who are hurt *do* react with anger! Denial of feelings is evident here.

19. This person truly is afraid of his or her emotions and, because of this, shuts out life.

20. Here we have a person who is in need of proving himself or herself. There is a need to feel important and a resentment of others who want to live their own lives.

21. Persons who use this approach are manipulators. By heaping praise, they hope to snare someone into doing some job for them.

Scoring Analysis: The reader will need to compare answers to those that have been provided. In some cases, half credits may be applied at the reader's discretion. General scoring categories are as follows:

Number Correct
- 0- 5   Poor Awareness
- 6-10   Average
- 11-15   Very Good
- 16-18   Excellent
- 19-21   A Born Psychologist

Conclusions: Now that you have completed this test, you have the means to evaluate how well you understand one facet of human behavior. If you scored poorly, you may want to develop your powers of drawing the other person out. Learning to ask the right question at the right time takes time. Don't expect quick improvement, but try harder to focus upon the other person. If you did well, you now know that you have knowledge of human behavior that can be used to strengthen your relationships. This knowledge can be powerful; be careful not to use it to judge others, because seeing deeply into others can pose a threat to them. For example, by stripping their defenses, you may make others feel uncomfortable and emotionally vulnerable.

The Conscience Test

Introduction: Do you feel that "liberating" an occasional pencil or postage stamp from the office isn't really stealing, because "everybody does it"? Do you believe that it is impossible for men and women to be guided by the same set of rules? Do you share the opinion that children today are confronted with more sexual temptations than when you were young? Would you consider cheating on this test by looking up the answers first?

The answers you give to these questions can help reveal your conscience type. In fact, a "yes" response to all four questions could reveal *four* different conscience types. The questions that follow will help you determine to which conscience type you are most closely allied. And this, in turn, can tell you some interesting things about your personality. You probably have heard the hoary joke about the puritanical New England conscience. It really doesn't stop them from doing anything sinful, it merely stops them from enjoying it after they have done it.

Know the conscience and you know the person? Not entirely. But your conscience very likely determines your tolerance of others, flexibility, emotional outlets, self-consistency, inner freedom and handling of guilt.

Do you, for example, become angry at others for doing that which you wish you could do? Do you seek vicarious risks and excitement through others—rooting, at the movies, for the criminals rather than the "good guys"? Do you habitually judge other people? This test will provide some insights into these conscience-dictated traits in your character—and the results will provide a revealing look at your controls, flexibility, expectations of others, concepts of discipline and many more important personality traits.

There have been voluminous articles and opinions about man's conscience. Yet, despite all of this attention, few persons are able to define what the conscience is. However, it is most interesting to see just what kind of conscience an individual has. The following test should aid in that goal.

Directions: To the following statements simply check whether you agree or disagree. There may be a number of statements with which you neither clearly agree nor disagree. Force yourself to make a choice, since avoidance impairs the test. Then read the scoring instructions to see how to evaluate your performance.

1. Very few persons can be trusted today.
    Agree   Disagree

2. We must set standards and then see that everyone follows them.
    Agree   Disagree

3. In order to insure honesty we must severely punish the dishonest.
    Agree   Disagree

4. There is always a clear line between right and wrong.
    Agree   Disagree

5. There is no excuse for the sexual behavior of people today.
    Agree   Disagree

6. Too much is made of police brutality.
    Agree   Disagree

7. I never could forgive one of my children for sexual immorality.
    Agree   Disagree

8. I suffer strong guilt when I do something I feel is wrong.
    Agree   Disagree

9. The values of yesterday are good enough for today.
    Agree   Disagree

10. If I had my way we would burn half of the books on the market today.
    Agree   Disagree

11. Fear is what keeps people controlled.
    Agree   Disagree

12. I have no sympathy for the troubles of our promiscuous youth.
    Agree   Disagree

13. I would be in favor of shooting looters.
    Agree   Disagree

14. We never can have the same rules for both men and women.
    Agree   Disagree

15. Surely God will punish those who behave immorally.
    Agree   Disagree

16. I never could forgive a transgression by my spouse.
    Agree   Disagree

17. One has the right to know about a spouse's background.
    Agree   Disagree

18. I could not associate with those whose values are greatly different from my own.
    Agree   Disagree

19. I would disown my daughter if she got pregnant illegitimately.
    Agree   Disagree

20. Some people are born bad.
    Agree   Disagree

21. People who are dishonest in one circumstance will be dishonest in most other circumstances.
    Agree   Disagree

22. It is wrong even to feel angry.
    Agree   Disagree

23. Punishment should fit the crime and not the causes.
    Agree   Disagree

24. It is best to hold most emotions inside.
    Agree   Disagree

25. I can't tolerate any transgression.
    Agree   Disagree

26. Everyone in the society steals.
    Agree   Disagree

27. If the majority do something, then it is right.
    Agree   Disagree

28. Stealing from large companies is not so bad because they can afford it.
    Agree   Disagree

29. Honesty seldom is the best policy.
    Agree   Disagree

30. Most people will take what they can.
    Agree   Disagree

31. The end justifies the means.
    Agree   Disagree

32. One has to put personal values aside in order to get ahead in the world.
    Agree   Disagree

33. Nearly any emotional outlet is better than none.
    Agree   Disagree

34. I probably would cheat if I could get away with it.
    Agree   Disagree

35. I break laws when I drive.
    Agree   Disagree

36. I set higher standards for others than I do for myself.
    Agree   Disagree

37. I knowingly falsify my income tax returns.
    Agree   Disagree

38. One must cheat on insurance claims.
    Agree   Disagree

39. Everyone steals something from the office.
    Agree   Disagree

40. Everyone lies much of the time.
    Agree   Disagree

41. I can't understand why people get so upset when someone lies.
    Agree   Disagree

42. Children have to be dishonest in school because it is such a competitive world.
    Agree   Disagree

43. Shoplifting is not the major crime that it is made out to be.
    Agree   Disagree

44. I can well understand why some of our leaders are physically attacked.
    Agree   Disagree

45. One should get ahead in life at all costs.
    Agree   Disagree

46. The best way to insure honesty in children is to set a good example as parents.
    Agree   Disagree

47. I do not like dishonesty because it hurts other people.
    Agree   Disagree

48. There are circumstances wherein most people would steal.
    Agree   Disagree

49. Today's youth has to face many sexual temptations that did not exist for earlier generations.
    Agree   Disagree

50. Not everyone has the same values.
    Agree   Disagree

51. Except for major crimes, we should be tolerant of the behavior of others.
    Agree   Disagree

52. My personal values change somewhat from time to time.
    Agree   Disagree

53. It is not always easy to decide between what is right and what is wrong.
    Agree   Disagree

54. We need more highly trained police officers.
    Agree   Disagree

55. Each person should act as his or her own censor with movies.
    Agree   Disagree

56. No one can judge the behavior of others unless he or she is in the same position.
    Agree   Disagree

57. Moral values undergo changes.
    Agree   Disagree

58. I worry more about my behavior than about the behavior of others.
    Agree   Disagree

59. I would expect my children to behave differently than we did when I was young.
    Agree   Disagree

60. People live by many different sets of values.
    Agree   Disagree

61. I am not in favor of harsh discipline.
    Agree   Disagree

62. Maturity provides a controlling mechanism.
    Agree   Disagree

63. Frequent rewards are good.
    Agree   Disagree

64. Honesty is an important personal value of mine.
    Agree   Disagree

65. I always try to be honest with my family.
    Agree   Disagree

66. A person who steals once will do it again.
    Agree   Disagree

67. We need more strict discipline.
    Agree   Disagree

68. Punishment should fit the crime.
    Agree   Disagree

69. People today are too sexually liberal.
    Agree   Disagree

70. I would not commit a crime because I would be afraid of being caught.
    Agree   Disagree

71. Women who wear revealing clothes are asking for trouble.
    Agree   Disagree

72. I pay all of my parking violations.
    Agree   Disagree

73. I frequently appraise my behavior to see that I am living up to my values.
    Agree   Disagree

74. I would penalize myself if I violated the rules of some contest.
    Agree   Disagree

75. I would never cheat on a questionnaire.
    Agree   Disagree

Scoring: Four conscience types are measured by this test. The first can be called the *Rigid Conscience*. This type is characterized by the attitude that right is right and there are no shades of gray. There is little or no flexibility with this kind of conscience and punishment is very harsh. The second type is termed the *Loose Conscience,* and this type is characterized by the philosophy that everyone should get away with as much as possible since nearly everyone is dishonest. The third, or *Flexible Conscience*, sets standards but considers the circumstances. Punishment is not harsh and controls are set mainly by a desire to be good to fellow mankind. The final type is the *Strict Conscience.* This type falls between the Flexible and Rigid types. Standards are very strong but some consideration is given to circumstances.

Few persons have a conscience built of only one type, but there is a tendency to lean in one direction. A profile is the best way to analyze the overall conscience pattern. To simplify scoring, the various types have been grouped as follows:

Questions 1 through 25 refer to the Rigid Conscience;
Questions 26 through 45 refer to the Loose Conscience;
Questions 46 through 65 refer to the Flexible Conscience;
Questions 66 through 75 refer to the Strict Conscience.

Count the number of "agree" answers that you have checked under each category. Then assign weighted values as follows:

1. Each "agree" answer for a Rigid Conscience counts 4%;
2. Each "agree" answer for a Loose Conscience counts 5%;
3. Each "agree" answer for a Flexible Conscience counts 5%;
4. Each "agree" answer for a Strict Conscience counts 10%.

For example, if you answered "agree" to five of the questions representing a *Loose Conscience* your total would be 25% for a Loose Conscience.

Profile of Conscience Types

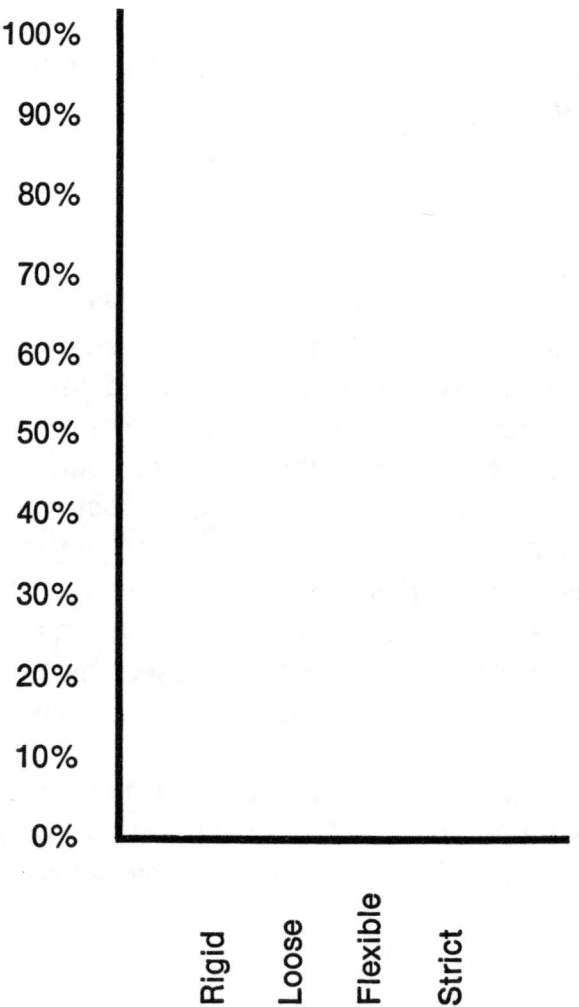

Conclusions: Once you have identified the type of conscience you have, you can evaluate any changes you feel to be desirable. Are you too hard on yourself or others? Are your controls so loose that you may offend others? If so, perhaps you need to evaluate those forces that helped shape your conscience. Maybe you need a restructuring to fit your current life situation.

The Manipulation Test

Introduction: Do you shape your own destiny? Do you generally control your own actions? Are you your own person? Do you make your own purchases or are you directed by others skilled in the art of manipulation? Are you a habitual winner or loser? These are vitally important questions for each of us to answer, especially today when so many are skilled in the art of manipulation.

All of us have to play different roles at various times, but the major question is, "who predominates?" This test will help you determine who controls your behavior. Do you, or does someone else? How susceptible are you to manipulation by others?

Directions: Our whole society today seems to be built upon some variety of manipulation. The question becomes one of how susceptible each of us is to this type of control. The following test should allow the reader to make a self-appraisal. Read each of the following questions, mark the appropriate answer and then check the analysis to see how you rate.

1. When people bombard you with their values, you:

a. find that your own values change.
b. accept their views as applicable to them.
c. ignore what they say at the time but later find yourself questioning your values.

2. If someone whom you feel is much brighter than you argues a point, you:

a. tend to yield rather quickly
b. consistently question that person.
c. find yourself slowly convinced.

3. If a friend asks you to do something you really dislike, you would:

a. grudgingly agree.
b. discuss your feelings and perhaps not do it.
c. complain but probably give in.

4. When you shop, do you:

a. find yourself attracted to the brightest package.
b. know specifically what you are looking for.
c. generally follow the advice of the clerk.

5. When buying a car, do you:

a. always go to one car dealer.
b. shop around.
c. buy from the salesperson who most logically presents a case for a particular automobile.

6. When a street beggar approaches you for money, you are likely to:

a. give him what he wants so he will leave you alone.
b. ignore him.
c. argue with him but give in if others with you do so.

7. A hostess at a party insists that you have yet another drink. You feel you have had enough. You are likely to:

a. take the drink so as not to offend her.
b. thank her but tell her you have had enough.
c. say "no," unless she persists.

8. If you told your child that he could not stay out at night and he said that other youngsters his age were still out, you would:

a. allow him to stay out.
b. tell him you are sorry but you feel he needs to come in.
c. check to see how many others are out and then perhaps allow him to remain out.

9. Another couple invites you to their house for dinner. You don't really want to go. You are likely to:

a. go, since you don't want to hurt their feelings.
b. tell them you have other plans.
c. try to find another excuse, but in the end, probably go.

10. A young neighbor wants to cut your grass. You don't like the job he does but he is insistent. You would:

a. let him do the job.
b. tell him you have someone else to do the job.
c. help him so he did a better job.

11. A friend wants to borrow a tool that you hate to lend. What would you do?

a. probably lend it anyway.
b. tell him that you need it.
c. try to convince him that you need it, but probably lend it to him.

12. A stockbroker tells you that he has a real hot stock. He has failed you in the past with these "hot tips." You would:

a. give him another chance.
b. tell him you have lost faith in "hot tips."
c. think it over, but then probably decide to take one more chance.

13. When people ask you to loan them money, you:

a. nearly always give in.
b. never give in.
c. sometimes give in.

14. When people ask your advice and you feel they may well get angry over what you tell them, you:

a. give it anyway.
b. let them decide the issue for themselves.
c. hold off until they persist.

15. When clothing styles change, do you:

a. change right with them.
b. decide for yourself what style looks best for you.
c. change after everyone else changes.

16. You see a number of people making fools of themselves at a party. They ask you to join in the game. You are likely to:

a. join in.
b. avoid such behavior.
c. wait until nearly everyone joins in.

17. A known reckless driver offers you a ride. Would you:

a. accept, but worry all the way.
b. refuse.
c. accept, but try to advise caution.

18. If someone complained that you generally do that which you feel is right for you, you would:

a. try to change.
b. accept the statement as a compliment.
c. argue, but probably see the error of your ways.

19. When you are with heavy drinkers generally you:

a. join in and drink heavily.
b. stay at your own level of drinking.
c. drink more than usual but try to slow them down.

20. You see a painting that you like. Others strongly criticize the painting. You would:

a. alter your opinion.
b. stick to your opinion.
c. still like the painting but not as much.

For Men Only

1. A group of men are talking badly about a woman you like. You would:

a. probably alter your opinion of her.
b. not change your opinion and perhaps even defend her reputation.
c. try to argue against them.

2. A driver scrapes the fender of your car. When the driver emerges from the car you note that she is most attractive. You would:

a. apologize for any initial anger.
b. tell her that she has damaged your car.
c. inform her that your insurance companies can settle it.

3. You have just put on a new sport coat that you have hitherto loved. An attractive lady doesn't like it. You are apt to:

a. get a new sport coat.
b. figure that she has a right to her opinion and you do to yours.
c. look for a second opinion.

4. A very attractive magazine saleslady is pushing some magazines that are not among your favorites. You probably would:

a. buy several magazines.
b. tell her you are not interested.
c. try to indicate that these magazines are not among your favorites.

5. You are waiting in line at a carry-out restaurant. A lady barges in front of you, saying she is rushed. You would:

a. smile and say nothing.
b. tell her you are sorry but you are rushed too.
c. try to persuade her that she should wait her turn, but not push it.

For Women Only

1. You have an argument with a man who indicates that you are using feminine logic. You would:

a. back off.
b. point out that he is not using logic.
c. listen to his points and probably yield.

2. You are not in a sexy mood. Your husband tells you that it has been a number of days since there had been any sexual activity. What would you do?

a. probably yield.
b. tell him you are sorry but that doesn't change your mood.
c. try to compromise and promise him you will be in the mood tomorrow.

3. There is a discussion about abortion. Several people attack the position you hold. You would:

a. probably yield because of the heavy emotionality.
b. stick to your guns.
c. yield only if their arguments seem immediately sound.

4. Your boss asks you to run an errand for him and you dislike this type of job. You try to get out of it but he says, "Oh well, then I'm afraid I will have to do it!" You would:

a. yield because of guilt feelings.
b. stick to your position.
c. try to convince him that it isn't that difficult for him to run the errand, but yield if he still feels it would be difficult for him.

5. You feel angry at a remark made to you at a party by another woman. A third person tells you that it isn't feminine to be angry. You would:

a. hold your anger in.
b. tell her you are still angry, maybe even more so after her comment.
c. try to convince her it is allowable for a woman to feel angry. If you succeed, then you may ventilate your feelings.

Scoring: This is a very easy test to self-score. Answer B in each case indicates that you resist manipulation by others. Count the number of times you select a B answer and rate yourself.

22-25	Manipulation Proof
18-21	Above Average
14-17	Average Mark
11-13	Far Below Average
10 and under	A Very Easy Target

In addition, check yourself as follows. Every A answer indicates easy manipulation, while each C answer shows that you can be manipulated but you offer token resistance.

Conclusion: Are you surprised by the results? If you do find that you are easily manipulated by others you may now understand why you often do things that you regret later. You may wish to explore books on self-assertiveness. At the other extreme, are you so individualized that you seem uncompromising to others? At least now you can make some choices.

The Personal Equation Test
(Are you Romantic, Sensual, or Practical?)

Introduction: Do you feel that business should always come before pleasure? Have you secretly yearned for great powers of attraction over the opposite sex? Are you a daydreamer? Do others accuse you of indifference to their personal needs?

Sometimes it may seem that two people involved in a relationship are pulling in opposing directions. One wants more "closeness and affection," while the other desires "great accomplishments in life." Arguments are likely to follow, with numerous complaints and accusations on each side. It is difficult to resolve any conflict until you see what it is that each person wants. The Personal Equation Test should go far toward revealing the desires of the person taking the test.

Directions: Circle the letter after the question that is descriptive of your feelings, desires, or behavior. The first twenty-one questions are for women only, the second twenty-one for men only.

For Women Only

1. Do you prefer personal gifts?   S

2. Do men frequently smile at you?   S

3. Do men think you are sexy?   S

4. Do you budget the money you spend on clothes?   P

5. Do you follow the stock market?   P

6. Do you diet to keep your figure?   S

7. Do you want your man to remember what you wore on special occasions?   R

8. Are you sensitive to the feelings of others?   R

9. Do you save letters written to you by your man?   R

10. Do you love intimate candlelight dinners?   R

11. Do you prefer casual clothing?   P

12. Do you love to receive flowers?   R

13. Do you like surprise gifts?   R

14. Do you love very fragrant perfumes?   S

15. Can you easily balance a check book?   P

16. Do you exercise regularly?   P

17. Do you enjoy moonlight?   S

18. Are you an avid reader?   P

19. Do you enjoy revealing clothes?   S

20. Do you love sports?   P

21. Do you have special songs that remind you of the past?   R

For Men Only

1. Do you pay special attention to your clothes?   S

2. Are you very aware of the feelings of others?   S

3. Do you like candlelight dinners?   S

4. Do you favor shirts open at the neck?   S

5. Do you like to "get away" with your woman?   R

6. Do you have special songs that remind you of your woman?   R

7. Do you buy perfume for your woman?   S

8. Are you a night person?   R

9. Do you enjoy having women look at you?   S

10. Is it difficult for you to spend money on yourself?   P

11. Do you like masculine aftershave colognes?   S

12. Do you carefully budget your money?   P

13. Do you like to write letters to the one you love?   R

14. Do you exercise regularly?   P

15. Do you buy a car mainly for the gas mileage it gives?   P

16. Do you buy mainly casual clothes?   P

17. Do you check your investments carefully?   P

18. Do you buy flowers for that special person?   R

19. Do you enjoy buying personal gifts for your lady?   R

20. Do you enjoy returning to restaurants that bring back
    special memories?   R

21. Does getting ahead in business mean a great deal to you?   P

Scoring: Count how many times you have circled each letter and then read what the letters stand for (below). The letter you have chosen most often will be most revealing of your personality. Some people choose all three letters equally or nearly equally. They are individuals with great emotional balance.

   The letters stand for the following:

S Type—sensitive, sensual, seductive persons fall in this grouping. Much awareness of bodily feelings and sensations and a strong emotional interest in the opposite sex.

R Type—typified by a romantic interest in others—sensitive to the feelings of others—deep interest in atmosphere and past happy memories.

P Type—persons who are practical, strong in business, interested in change and worldly success.

Conclusions: Perhaps the results of the test came as a surprise to you. You may want to compare your results with the results of your mate. That may help you find some of the key differences in your motivations. That, in turn, should allow for both compromise and understanding of what happens in your relationship.

2. Tests of Marital Adjustment

1. A Test of Marital Adjustment
2. A Test of Desired Changes
3. How Well Do You Know Your Mate?
4. The Affairs Test—For Women Only
5. The Affairs Test—For Men Only

It is important to recognize that there are no perfect marriages. The best are those that continue to show growth and development. Weak areas need constant improvement and these tests should help point up areas of discontent.

Of even greater importance is mutual understanding. As that takes place, we usually can share more and communicate better. Stronger marriages generally go hand in hand with improved communication. These tests were particularly designed to be shared with a loved one. So, in a spirit of fun, begin sharing the tests that lie ahead.

A Test of Marital Adjustment

Introduction: A friend once told me that he had the ideal marriage and I offered my congratulations. Six months later, he was involved with the divorce courts. Apparently, his wife didn't think it ideal. With nearly half of all marriages ending in divorce, it behooves all of us to take a periodic look at our marital adjustment. Generally, problems do not develop overnight and, in many cases, they could have been handled at the onset of the problem. Unfortunately, many people wait too long. As a result, hostility builds up and communication is lost.

It may be that good marriages are fashioned in heaven, but it still takes abundant amounts of work on earth to make them tick! However, if one cannot identify the weak spots, it may be impossible to know where to begin the effort. Take a look at how you might rate your marriage. Perhaps you can compare notes with your spouse and improve those lines of communication.

Instructions: Answer "yes" or "no" to the following questions and then check the scoring procedures at the conclusion of the questions.

1. Do you and your mate agree on the number of children you want?
   Yes   No

2. Is there family agreement on the discipline of children?
   Yes   No

3. Do you feel that your mate loves you as much as you love him or her?
   Yes   No

4. Do you feel affectionate toward your mate?
   Yes   No

5. Does your mate show you adequate affection?
   Yes   No

6. Do you generally feel relaxed and accepted by your mate?
   Yes   No

7. Are you able to request changes in your sexual life?
   Yes   No

8. Are you satisfied with the frequency of your sexual outlet?
   Yes   No

9. Are the sexual practices in which you engage with your mate appealing to you?
   Yes   No

10. When there are conflicts can you talk about them?
    Yes   No

11. When you talk, do you feel that your mate understands what you are saying?
    Yes   No

12. Are you free to ask your mate for things that you would like?
    Yes   No

13. Do you feel that your mate is interested in your feelings?
    Yes   No

14. Has the marriage helped you to grow and develop your own talents?
    Yes   No

15. Do marital fights frequently lead to improved communication?
    Yes   No

16. Do you ever laugh off disagreements after they are resolved?
    Yes   No

17. Do you generally understand what your mate is saying?
    Yes   No

18. Have you been significantly more depressed since you married?
    Yes   No

19. Do you or your mate nag one another frequently?
    Yes   No

20. Are you or your spouse heavy drinkers?
    Yes   No

21. Do you feel that your mate and you also are good friends?
    Yes   No

22. Does your mate respect your opinion?
    Yes   No

23. Were (or are) both partners able to plan when they want children?
    Yes   No

24. Do things improve after you talk about them?
    Yes   No

25. Do you and your mate have similar views about life?
    Yes   No

26. Do you and your mate sometimes just talk about things in general?
    Yes   No

27. Are most verbal arguments with your mate rational?
    Yes   No

28. Can you generally sense what your mate wants?
    Yes   No

29. Do you find that your sexual life has gradually improved over the years?
    Yes   No

30. Are you free to initiate sexual interaction?
    Yes   No

31. Are you able to talk to your mate about future goals?
    Yes   No

32. When there are fights do you feel psychologically destroyed?
    Yes   No

33. Are your arguments with your mate generally vicious?
    Yes   No

34. Have you never had an argument?
    Yes   No

35. Has your own identity been lost in the marriage?
    Yes   No

36. Do you have variety in your sex life?
    Yes   No

37. Is there agreement on the type of relationships and activities that exist outside of the marriage?
    Yes   No

38. Does your mate feel proud of your accomplishments?
    Yes   No

39. Do you have strong feelings of loneliness?
    Yes   No

40. Does your mate complain about your sexual technique?
    Yes   No

41. Do both of you share the child-rearing responsibilities?
    Yes   No

42. Can both partners plan the spending of money?
    Yes   No

43. Is there general agreement on the style of living?
    Yes   No

44. Do you take vacations that are planned by both partners?
    Yes   No

45. Do you agree with the type and quantity of family entertainment?
    Yes   No

46. Are you generally able to meet your mate's expectations?
    Yes   No

47. Are you and your spouse mutually able to share opinions on different topics?
    Yes   No

48. Do you feel generally dominated by your mate?
    Yes   No

49. Are feelings of jealousy common in your marriage?
    Yes   No

50. Do you have major problems with in-laws?
    Yes   No

Scoring: There are 12 "no" answers and all of the remainder should be answered "yes." The "no" answers are 18, 19, 20, 32, 33, 34, 35, 39, 40, 48, 49, 50.

A point system for correct answers is as follows:

Questions 1 through 20	10 points
Questions 21 through 35	8 points
Questions 36 through 40	7 points
Questions 41 through 50	5 points

Rating Your Adjustment:

380-405	Excellent Adjustment
360-379	Above Average
340-359	About Average
330-339	Below Average
320-329	Well Below Average
319 and under	Some Significant Conflicts

If your score is low or leaves you unsatisfied, you might do well to look at the weak areas and see if improvement can't be made. Each person, however, has to judge what he or she wants and can accept or live with. Perhaps you can compare results with your mate and work together on desired changes.

Conclusion: Hopefully, as you talk, you will find that the marriage improves because of the interest each partner shows. Showing your spouse that you do care is a good part of the battle. If things do not improve, you may wish to seek professional help.

A Test of Desired Changes
(What You Would Like To Change In Yourself And In Your Mate)

Introduction: Do you subscribe to the theory that everyone, at least secretly, dislikes something about themselves? Does it seem accurate to say that to be human is to complain, to find fault? Are you a person who makes New Year's resolutions, who enjoys making a fresh start? Most of us feel some self-dissatisfaction but the feeling usually is vague and the desired new direction unclear.

When it comes to a mate, however, most people clearly know they would like changes made. They push and prod but, again, the direction is unclear. I once worked with a man who claimed that his wife was "too fat." So she lost weight. Was he then satisfied? Not at all! He then claimed that she was "too thin." She, on the other hand, complained that he was intolerant and "complains too much."

This test was constructed to help you determine the kinds of changes you really want. Change can't take place until you are able to pinpoint the direction of change. This test is designed to help couples do just that—and also to bring their gripes out into the open. From there, maybe bargains can be made!

Instructions: First answer each statement that indicates a change you would like to make in yourself. Then proceed with the second list and respond to the statements by indicating changes you would like your mate to make in himself or herself. Then analyze the results according to the directions that are provided at the conclusion of the test.

A.
1. I would like to be thinner.
2. I am not happy with my body build.
3. I would like to have a more solid body build.
4. I would like to look sexier in my clothes.
5. I would like to be more physically attractive.

B.
1. I worry too much.
2. Too many things bother me.
3. I am too intense.
4. I am too often depressed.
5. I am too dependent.
6. I would like to feel more confident.
7. I would like to be more comfortable when I am alone.
8. I would like to feel more joyful.
9. I would like to feel more aggressive.
10. I would like to feel more optimistic.

C.
1. I lose my temper too much.
2. I express emotion with too much intensity.
3. I am too often moved to tears.
4. I am too sarcastic.
5. Most of the time I hold feelings in too much.
6. I would like to be able to talk out feelings more.
7. I wish I could express emotion more directly.
8. I would like to be more spontaneous.

D.

1. I am too impulsive.
2. I am too careless.
3. I am too jealous of others.
4. I am too cautious.
5. I am too perfectionistic.
6. I take life too seriously.

E.

1. I can't get others to talk to me.
2. Frequently, I have difficulty in understanding what others are saying.
3. I would like to talk more with others.
4. I wish I could communicate better with others.
5. I don't know how to tell other people how I feel about them.
6. I can't put my feelings into words.

F.

1. I am too shy.
2. I don't feel sufficiently comfortable with strangers.
3. I would like to be more sociable.
4. I would like to be more outgoing.
5. I wish I could enjoy large parties more than I do.

G.

1. I would like to have more close friends.
2. I wish I could open myself up more to intimates.
3. I would like to be more romantic with my mate.
4. I would like to do more things with my mate.
5. I would like to spend more time with my family.
6. I wish I were closer with my children.

H.

1. I brag too much with friends.
2. I am too jealous of friends and loved ones.
3. My feelings are too easily hurt by those with whom I am very close.
4. I am too passive with people to whom I feel very close.
5. I am too dominating with friends and loved ones.

I.

1. I wish I felt my future looked brighter.
2. I do not handle money well.
3. My individuality is not well developed.
4. I would like to be more physically active.
5. I wish I could feel more important as a result of my work.
6. I would like to be more creative.
7. I would like to be able to try new forms of entertainment.
8. I would like to be more knowledgeable about the world.

J.

1. I would like more physical closeness.
2. I would like more variety in my sexual life.
3. I would like to be more sexually responsive.
4. I wish I was more sexually giving.
5. I want to be more sexually aggressive.
6. I wish I had more capacity for love-making.

Now answer each statement that indicates a change you would like your mate to be able to make.

A. I wish my mate:
1. were thinner.
2. could change his or her body build.
3. had a more solid build.
4. looked sexier in his or her clothes.
5. was more physically attractive.

B. I wish my mate:

1. didn't worry so much.
2. didn't let so many things bother him or her.
3. was not so intense.
4. was not so often depressed.
5. was not so dependent.
6. felt more self confident.
7. felt more comfortable when he or she is alone.
8. was more joyful.
9. could be more aggressive.
10. felt more optimistic.

C. My mate:

1. loses his or her temper too much.
2. expresses emotion with too much intensity.
3. is too often moved to tears.
4. is too sarcastic.
5. holds in too much his or her feelings.
6. needs to talk out more of his or her feelings.
7. should be able to express emotion more directly.
8. needs to be more spontaneous.

D. My mate is:

1. too impulsive.
2. too careless.
3. too jealous of others.
4. too cautious.
5. too perfectionistic.
6. apt to take life too seriously.

E. My mate:

1. usually can't get others to talk to her or him.
2. frequently has difficulty in understanding what others are saying.
3. should want others to talk more with him or her.
4. doesn't know how to tell others how he or she feels about them.
5. should be more adept at communicating with others.

F. My mate:
1. is too shy.
2. doesn't feel sufficiently comfortable with strangers.
3. needs to be more sociable.
4. needs to be more outgoing.
5. needs to be able to enjoy large parties more than he or she does.

G. I wish my mate:
1. had more close friends.
2. could open up more.
3. could be more romantic with me.
4. liked to do more things with me.
5. spent more time with our family.
6. was closer to our children.

H. My mate:
1. brags too much with friends.
2. is too jealous of friends and loved ones.
3. has his or her feelings hurt too easily by those very close to him or her.
4. is too passive with people very close to him or her.
5. is too dominating with friends and loved ones.

I. My mate:
1. needs to see a brighter future for himself or herself.
2. does not handle money well.
3. does not have well developed individuality.
4. should be more physically active.
5. should feel more important in his or her work.
6. should be more creative.
7. should be able to try new forms of entertainment.
8. should be more knowledgeable about the world.

J. I wish my mate:
1. liked more physical closeness.
2. liked greater variety in our sexual life.
3. was more sexually responsive.
4. was more sexually giving.
5. was more sexually aggressive.
6. had a greater capacity for love-making.

Scoring: If you graph the results of this test you readily will identify those areas that demand the greatest attention. It is particularly important to see how much overlap there is between desired changes for self and the desired changes for your mate. This will show at a glance whether a spouse wishes his or her mate to be more like him or her or whether there are feelings of overlapping weakness. From that point, a couple should be able to compare notes and see what changes each would like made. As the communication improves, so too may the relationship. Talking is the first step to growth.

It is suggested that readers construct a bar graph and note the areas with the greatest emphasis for both partners. A line in pen can designate the self changes while a pencil line can be used for desired changes in the mate. The graph should be set up as follows:

Profile of Desired Changes

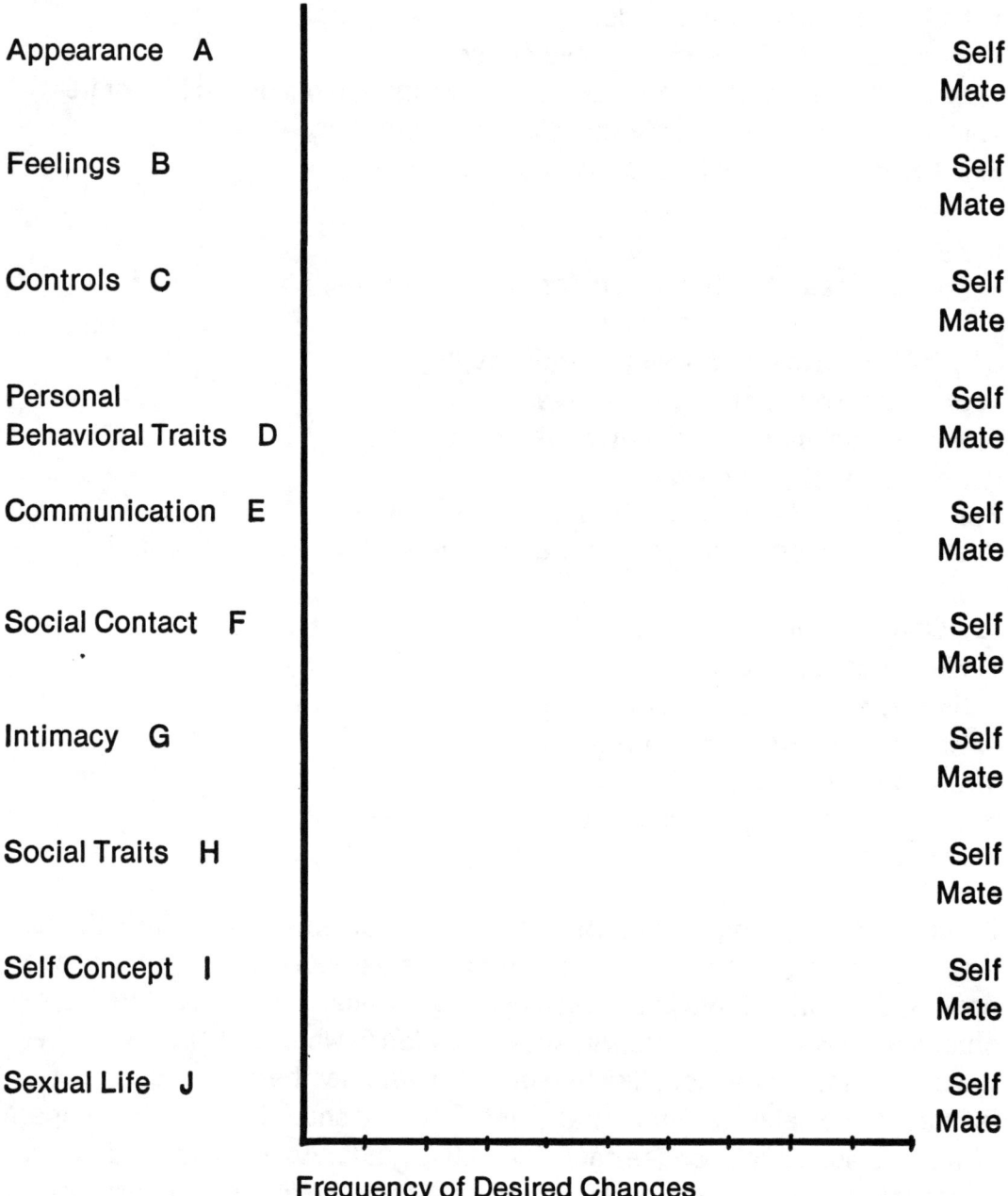

Frequency of Desired Changes

How Well Do You Know Your Mate?

Introduction: So you think you know your lover! Many persons have made this confident claim, only to be shocked later by some previously unknown behavioral tendency or desire. One of the more surprising factors revealed by marital counseling is how often two people are alike and yet unaware of this similarity. In many cases, a couple may have quarreled for years over alleged differences, only to find at the counselor's office that they shared more than they thought.

It is very difficult to share something with a lover unless you know what that person really wants—and that requires knowledge of your loved one. This test will help you evaluate your knowledge of your lover, and vice versa. Armed with that information, you each may find that the sharing of life's joys increases.

Directions: Answer each question two ways: first as you think your mate would answer, next as you would answer relating the question to yourself. Do not show your answers to your mate until he or she has indicated his or her choices. Then check the scoring procedures to see how you have done. One additional point: Out of fairness, both partners should take the test to see how they compare.

What would you say is your mate's:

1. favorite food?
2. favorite cocktail?
3. favorite after-dinner drink?
4. favorite dessert?
5. favorite mood music?
6. favorite singer?
7. favorite dance music?
8. favorite type of book?
9. favorite kind of movie?
10. most preferred movie star?
11. least favorite movie star?
12. favorite spectator sport?
13. favorite participating sport?
14. favorite relaxing pastime?
15. favorite vacation activity?
16. favorite vacation sport?
17. favorite non-athletic game?
18. favorite make of car?
19. favorite type of gift?
20. favorite form of correspondence?

Which of the following would your mate prefer:

21.
a. making love at home in bed?
b. making love in front of a fire?
c. making love in a car?
d. making love in a motel?

22.
a. introverted people?
b. shy people?
c. extroverted people?

23.
a. large parties with a number of strangers?
b. large parties with friends?
c. small parties with intimate friends?

24.
a. very casual clothes?
b. dress clothes?
c. work clothes?

25.
a. showers?
b. baths?
c. saunas?

26.
a. competition?
b. cooperative ventures?
c. solitary activities?

27.
a. indoor work?
b. outdoor work?
c. a combination of both?

28.
a. passive people?
b. assertive people?
c. dynamic people?

29.
a. talking to one close friend?
b. giving a speech?
c. debating some issue?

30.
a. a quiet evening at home?
b. an evening dancing?
c. dining out?

31.
a. well-planned tours?
b. spontaneous travel?
c. time spent at one location?

32.
a. an assertive sexual partner?
b. a passive sexual partner?
c. a compliant sexual partner?

33.
a. saving money?
b. investing money?
c. spending money?

34.
a. buying a home?
b. buying a car?
c. buying a boat?

35.
a. taking a test?
b. administering a test to someone else?
c. scoring a test?

36.
a. buying an intimate gift for a loved one?
b. receiving and intimate gift?
c. helping others buy gifts?

37.
a. Christmas?
b. New Years?
c. Easter?

38.
a. early morning?
b. midday?
c. late night?

39.
a. slapstick humor?
b. subtle humor?
c. insult humor?

40.
a. solitude at home?
b. solitude at the beach?
c. solitude in the woods?

41.
a. spring?
b. fall?
c. summer?

42.
a. hot weather?
b. cool weather?
c. temperate weather?

43.
a. mountainous terrain?
b. flat land?
c. gently sloping land?

44.
a. a small family?
b. a medium-sized family?
c. a large family?

45.
a. making decisions entirely on one's own?
b. shared decision making?
c. relying upon the judgement of others?

Which of following best describes your mate's behavior?

46.
a. seldom dreams at night?
b. frequently dreams at night?
c. sometimes dreams at night?

47.
a. enjoys new experiences?
b. takes what is tried and true?
c. seeks new experiences?

48.

a. often jokes with others?
b. generally is serious?
c. frequently is the target of jokes?

49.

a. seeks leadership roles?
b. avoids leadership roles?
c. accepts leadership roles when they are offered?

50.

a. is very relaxed after love making?
b. is very talkative after love making?
c. is very serious after love making?

Scoring: Each partner should take this test two ways: once to describe himself or herself and once to describe his or her partner. Answers then should be compared. There are fifty questions and each counts two percentage points. If a wife, for example, selects forty of the same answers as her husband she has scored 80%. She then can note how well her husband did in anticipating her answers, but let's keep it fun and be gracious winners and losers.

    90-100   percent is near perfection
    80- 89   percent is excellent
    70- 79   percent is very good

The Affairs Test—For Women Only

Introduction: At some point in their married lives, most women express concern that they have lost or are losing their man to a rival. They are convinced that the real or imagined lover has some special quality that they lack. I have found that in the counselor's office imaginations frequently run wild. There is much speculation about the "other woman," and many patients say, "I wish I knew what I was competing with." It seems that the fear of the unknown hangs heavy over the heads of these troubled women. What is this mysterious rival like? "What would my man find attractive?" women often ask.

    The Affairs Test helps draw out your ideas of what might turn your man on. To successfully complete this test, you must give free rein to your imagination. The authors of this test are not suggesting that your man is having an affair; he does, after all, have you. However, for the sake of this test you must *imagine* that your man *might* have an affair. Use your imagination to develop a picture of the rival by answering the questions provided. Then note the instructions for the second part of the test and conclude by checking the scoring. Remember, though, it is pure fun and fantasy.

For Women Only

Instructions: This is intended to be a fun test, but you will doubtless find it surprisingly informative too. Select the answer you consider best for each of the following questions.

1. How old would she probably be?

a. Under twenty
b. Twenty-one to thirty
c. Thirty-one to forty

2. What hair color is she likely to have?

a. Blond
b. Brunette
c. Red
d. Gray

3. How is she likely to wear her hair?

a. Casual
b. Long and flowing
c. Short

4. What would be her body type? (check one in each category)

a. Tall
b. Medium
c. Short

and
d. Thin
e. Slender
f. Heavy

5. What sort of figure would she have? (check one in each category)

a. Very busty
b. Medium bust
c. Small bust

d. Wide hips
e. Narrow hips
f. Medium hips

g. Slender legs
h. Heavy legs
i. Medium legs

6. How would she dress?

a. Casually
b. Very prim and proper
c. Seductively

7. What would her education be?

a. High school
b. College
c. Business school

8. What would her occupation be?

a. Professional
b. Housewife
c. Secretary
d. Nurse
e. Airline Stewardess
f. Advertising
g. Executive
h. Sales
i. Teacher

9. How would she function occupationally?

a. As a leader
b. As a follower
c. As a creative person
d. As a doer for others

10. How important would her vocation be?

a. A major portion of her life
b. Not nearly as important as her lover's
c. Only a minor portion of her life

11. What conversational approach would she use?

a. Mainly as a listener
b. Listening and questioning
c. A very active talker

12. About what is she likely to talk?

a. Her feelings for her lover
b. The future
c. Her lover's interests

13. Would she most often talk about

a. Sex
b. Her problems in life
c. Her lover's problems
d. Business
e. Entertainment

14. How would she probably communicate?

a. Verbally
b. Emotionally
c. By actions

15. How talkative is she likely to be?

a. Very talkative
b. Generally quiet
c. Talkative only in response to others

16. Of the following, which traits probably would most accurately describe her personality?

a. Exciting
b. Stimulating
c. Sympathetic
d. Empathetic

17. Which of these traits would describe her?

a. Quiet
b. A dreamer
c. A planner

18. She might be described as:

a. Dependent
b. Very independent
c. Very secure about herself

19. Her predominant mood would be:

a. very serious about life
b. nearly always gay and hopeful
c. very casual and carefree

20. Her style of humor would be:

a. a very subtle sense of humor
b. subdued
c. mainly enjoying the humor of others

21. She could be described in general as:

a. Passive
b. Aggressive
c. Dominant
d. Mixed passive and assertive

22. How would she be likely to handle her anger?

a. generally by holding it in
b. by talking it out in a direct manner
c. by giving in to others who caused it

23. She would handle her excitement by:

a. subduing it and thereby showing only traces of it
b. spontaneous outcries
c. verbal discussion

24. In general her feelings would be:

a. shared with others
b. shared only with her lover
c. generally subdued

25. If disappointed, she would be likely to:

a. complain a great deal
b. tell no one
c. show it by her mood change

26. Sexually, she is likely to be:

a. hard to get
b. subtly seductive
c. blatantly seductive

27. During sexual interaction she would:

a. have rich sexual fantasies
b. think only of her lover
c. not think of anything

28. Sexually, she is likely to be:

a. Aggressive
b. Hard to get
c. Responsive
d. Timid

29. Where sex is concerned she probably would be:

a. direct by talking about it openly
b. manipulative and coy
c. gracious and supportive of all that her lover does

30. She would be likely to make my mate feel:

a. guilty and indebted to her
b. very manly and aggressive
c. alive and passionate

31. She would be most likely to view men as:

a. father figures and heroes
b. kind and considerate
c. friends as well as lovers

32. The main thing she would likely share with my mate would be:

a. understanding
b. sex
c. a feeling of daring and adventure

33. The next most important shared activity would be:

a. talking
b. companionship
c. casual fun

34. She would most likely also share with my mate (select two):

a. an interest in his work
b. a strong sexual desire
c. an interest in outdoor activities
d. romantic interludes

35. Her attitude would help my mate:

a. feel young
b. feel sexually aggressive
c. feel wanted

36. If my mate wanted sex and she didn't she would most likely:

a. refuse
b. give in at once
c. give in after a token resistance

37. My mate and she likely would share:
a. primarily sex
b. an ability to communicate
c. an ability to experiment

38. Where sex is concerned, she would be:

a. somewhat jealous of other woman
b. never jealous of others
c. occasionally jealous of other women

39. If my mate was not in a sexy mood, she would:

a. accept his mood
b. become quietly irritated
c. gently try to change his mood

40. If there were time when my mate was not highly responsive, she would:

a. be highly supportive
b. become quiet
c. need reassurance that she was not to blame

Second Part of Test: Now go through the list of questions and select the answer that best describes yourself and your relationship with your mate.

Scoring: After completing this test you should have made 44 selections describing your would-be rival and 44 selections describing yourself. The object is to compare the two lists of answers to see how you compare to the mythical woman. It is important, however, to realize that no two people ever match perfectly. The question is how close you feel you are to the woman your spouse might select. Score the match-up as follows: Number of items matching from two lists of answers:

40-44	virtually perfect; he won't look around
35-39	a good match; an affair is unlikely
29-34	an average match-up
24-28	you are still close to one another
18-23	better check the areas of dissimilarity
17 and under	either make some changes or keep a close eye on him!

Conclusions: Now you have identified the enemy, real or imagined. You have codified that which you feel that your man would find attractive. Meet the enemy and she will be yours: *You can* become that woman—probably with very few changes. Or perhaps you will come to the realization that your concerns are unrealistic—your man and you are well matched!

For Men Only

Introduction: Have you ever thought that your woman might be seeing another man? Jealousy tends to creep into most male-female relationships. From the man's point of view, there seems to be increased concern due to the liberation of women. No longer is the lady found safely at home. Now, she often has her own career and that brings her into daily contact with men. Added to this is the new assertiveness of today's woman, the trend for women to seek more vigorously that which they want.

All of these factors add to a man's insecurities, suspicions and concerns. "What would the guy be like?" Men often wonder about the potential rival. This test will help you find out what you might be up against. You may literally be able to see your rival in your mind's eye.

To take this test, you must put aside your suspicions and use your imagination. Take the test in a spirit of fun and simply *imagine* that your lady *might* have an affair. Remember, this is pure fantasy. You are seeking only to develop a picture of what the other man might be like—if there was another man.

Instructions: Imagine that your mate might have an affair. What would the man be like? Answer each of the questions by selecting the characteristic that you feel in your imagination would best describe him. Then, following the instructions, take the second part of the test. Scoring will immediately follow the last question.

1. How old is he likely to be?

a. under 25
b. 25 to 35
c. 35-45

2. What is his hair color likely to be?

a. gray
b. dark
c. blond
d. medium

3. How would he wear his hair?

a. long
b. medium
c. crew cut
d. short

4. What would be his body type? (check one in each category)

a. tall
b. medium
c. short

d. thin
e. muscular
f. heavy

5. What sort of body characteristics would he have? (check one in each category)

a. wide shoulders
b. medium shoulders
c. slender shoulders

d. hairy chest
e. little body hair
f. medium body hair

6. How would he dress?

a. casually
b. open neck shirts
c. very stylishly
d. businesslike

7. What would his education be?

a. high school
b. college
c. business school
d. post graduate

8. What would his occupation be?

a. professional
b. business
c. artistic
d. service oriented
e. advertising
f. manual labor
g. political

9. How would he function occupationally?

a. as a leader
b. as a follower
c. as a creative person
d. as a doer for others

10. How important would his vocation be for him?

a. the major portion of his life
b. only as a means of earning money
c. important but secondary to his lover

11. What conversational approach would he use?

a. mainly as a listener
b. listening and questioning
c. seductive
d. argumentative and aggressive

12. What is he most likely to talk about?

a. work
b. his love for his lover
c. poetry
d. the future

13. Which would be likely to be his most common subject?

a. sex
b. his problems
c. his lover's problems
d. business
e. entertainment

14. In what manner would he communicate?

a. verbally
b. emotionally
c. by actions

15. How talkative would he likely be?

a. very talkative
b. talkative only in response to others
c. on the quiet side

16. Which of these common traits would best describe his personality?

a. exciting
b. stimulating
c. sympathetic
d. empathetic

17. Which of these traits would best describe him?

a. quiet
b. loving
c. a dreamer
d. a planner

18. He might be described as:

a. dependent
b. highly independent
c. very secure about himself

19. His predominant mood would be:

a. very serious about life
b. nearly always gay and hopeful
c. very casual and carefree

20. His style of humor would be:

a. subtle
b. subdued
c. insulting others
d. mainly enjoying the humor of others

21. He could be described as:

a. passive
b. aggressive
c. dominant
d. mixed passive and assertive

22. How would he handle his excitement?

a. by subduing it and thereby showing only traces of it
b. by direct, spontaneous expression
c. by verbal discussion

23. He would handle his anger by:

a. holding it in
b. talking it out in a direct manner
c. giving in to others
d. displaying a bad temper

24. In general, his feelings would be:

a. freely shared with others
b. shared only with his lover
c. generally subdued

25. If disappointed, he would likely:

a. complain a great deal
b. not tell anyone
c. show mood changes
d. talk it out

26. Sexually, he is likely to be:

a. direct and aggressive
b. subtly seductive
c. a little standoffish
d. quietly manipulative

27. During sexual interaction he would:

a. have rich sexual fantasies
b. follow the lead of his lover
c. initiate new practices

28. Sexually, he is likely to be:

a. timid
b. passive
c. aggressive
d. bold
e. responsive

29. Where sex is concerned, probably he would be:

a. *direct by openly talking about it*
b. *manipulative*
c. *gracious and supportive*
d. *tender and loving*

30. He would make my mate feel:

a. *alive and passionate*
b. *important*
c. *sexy*
d. *womanly and feminine*

31. He most likely would view women as:

a. *mainly sexual partners*
b. *friends*
c. *mother figures*
d. *friends as well as lovers*

32. The main thing he would share with my mate is:

a. *understanding*
b. *sex*
c. *a feeling of daring and adventure*

33. The next most important shared activity would be:

a. *talking*
b. *companionship*
c. *casual fun*

34. He and my mate mainly would share:

a. *an interest in his work*
b. *a strong sexual desire*
c. *an interest in outdoor activities*
d. *romantic interludes*

35. His attitude would help my mate:

a. *feel young*
b. *feel sexually aggressive*
c. *feel wanted*
d. *feel important*

36. If my mate wanted sex and he didn't, he most likely would:

a. refuse
b. give in at once
c. eventually give in
d. let her know it was his decision to make

37. My mate and he likely would share:

a. basically sex
b. an ability to communicate
c. an ability to experiment

38. Where sex is concerned, he would be:

a. somewhat jealous of other men
b. never jealous of others
c. occasionally jealous of others

39. If my mate was not in a sexy mood, he would:

a. accept her mood
b. become quietly irritated
c. gently try to change her mood

40. If there were times when my mate was not highly responsive, he would:
a. be highly supportive
b. become quiet
c. need reassurance that he was not to blame

41. If it was up to him, they would make love:
a. at our house
b. in a motel
c. outdoors when possible
d. in a car

42. After making love he would:

a. become very quiet
b. fall asleep
c. abruptly leave
d. remain affectionate

Second Part of the Test: Now go through the list of questions and select the answer that best describes yourself and your relationship with your mate.

Scoring: After completing this test you should have made 44 selections describing your rival and 44 selections describing yourself. The object is to compare the two lists of answers to see how you compare to the mythical man. It is important, however, to realize that no two people ever match perfectly. The question is how close you feel you are to the man your spouse might select. Score the match-up as follows:
Number of items matching from two lists of answers:
- 40-44   virtually perfect; she won't look around
- 35-39   a good match; an affair is unlikely
- 29-34   an average match-up
- 24-28   you still are close to one another
- 18-23   better check the areas of dissimilarity
- 17 and under   either make some changes or keep a close eye on her!

Conclusions: Now you have an idea of the type of battle, real or imagined, that you face. Is there really need for concern? Only you can determine that. However, is there really any reason why you can't make some changes and become that "other man"? It might be fun to compare test results and see what both of you would like. Then neither of you will have to spend time looking around.

3. Intelligence Tests

1. The Vocabulary Test
2. A Test of Abstract Intelligence
3. The Proverb Test
4. The Creative Intelligence Test

The tests that are included in this section are designed to give you an idea of your intellectual functioning. It is important to remember that an intelligence quotient (IQ) actually is composed of many different abilities. We no longer consider there to be only one IQ score that would indicate a person's intelligence.

These tests, however, provide a good measure of verbal and reasoning ability. These are areas important to many different kinds of problem-solving. It must be recognized, however, that these tests probably will not have the validity of an individual evaluation by a professional.

Introduction: Most of us have wondered from time to time how bright we are. Sometimes we hear words in conversation with which we are unfamiliar, but we hate to admit that lack of knowledge. We may secretly wonder how our vocabulary stacks up against others. Do you have the word-flexibility to make interesting conversation or do you use the same words with boring repetitiousness? **The Vocabulary Test** should answer those questions.

Abstract Intelligence is an ability to understand something that is complex and symbolic. This is another aspect of intelligence and this test offers us the chance to see where we stand. Can we really communicate with others? Can we follow complex instructions? **The Test of Abstract Intelligence** can provide answers.

The Proverb Test probes into another area of intellectual functioning. Do you, for example, understand subtle humor? Do you get the main point behind great literature? Do you understand what is written between the lines, so to speak? Do you see hidden meanings? The Proverb Test should add to your knowledge about yourself.

The Creative Intelligence Test will provide a measure of your intellectual flexibility. Can you find new solutions for problems? Can you use available facts in different combinations? Are you truly creative? Do you enjoy problem-solving? Can you apply your intelligence as well as most other people do? The Creative Intelligence Test can help find your intellectual uniqueness and show how you compare with others.

Should the results not be to your liking, all is not lost. There are books on building word knowledge, on developing abstract thinking, on logic and problem-solving. When you see your weak areas, you know where to begin in strengthening your intellect. It is not a matter of arguing over raising your so-called IQ. It is a fact that almost no one uses all of his or her intellectual resources. You can, with study, improve your intellectual functioning, but you need to know where your weaknesses are.

The Vocabulary Test

Instructions: Write what you consider to be the best definitions for the words that follow. Try to keep your definitions short; a number of mutually opposite words should not be considered correct. Then evaluate your performance by the standards provided on the next page.

1. money	12. alter	23. articulate	34. surreptitious
2. car	13. formulate	24. orifice	
3. coat	14. irregular	25. empathy	
4. brick	15. agitate	26. ludicrous	
5. couch	16. fabricate	27. enmity	
6. pen	17. discriminate	28. esoteric	
7. doctor	18. condone	29. vociferous	
8. knife	19. impending	30. pusillanimous	
9. impartial	20. diligent	31. parsimonious	
10. clarify	21. tenacity	32. acrimonious	
11. hesitate	22. stipulate	33. superfluous	

Scoring: Check your answers against the definitions below, and score each answer 0, 1 or 2. Give yourself a one-point score whenever you have used two words that are mutually opposite. Obviously, you will have to use your best judgment in determining how each answer is scored. Then total your score and rate as follows:

Score	Rating
14-17	borderline
18-24	dull normal
25-30	low average
31-37	average
38-44	above average
45-52	superior
53-60	very superior
61-68	gifted

Word Definitions
1. money—a coin or currency of exchange; certificates of exchange.
2. car—a vehicle moved on wheels; automobile.
3. coat—an article of clothing, generally outer garment; fur, skin of an animal.
4. brick—a unit of building material made by molding clay and then hardening by heat.
5. couch—a bed or structure for repose; sofa.
6. pen—an instrument for writing.
7. doctor—an advanced academic title; one who treats others for some illness.
8. knife—a cutting blade or tool.
9. impartial—unbiased, equitable, fair, just.
10. clarify—to make clear or more readily understandable.
11. hesitate—to be uncertain as to a course of action; to pause undecidedly.
12. alter—to change or make different.
13. formulate—to reduce to formula; systematize.
14. irregular—not fitting a pattern; not according to established rules.
15. agitate—to stir up or excite; perturb; set or keep in motion; make angry.
16. fabricate—to construct or build; to invent.
17. discriminate—to make a distinction; to favor one over others; to distinguish.

18. condone—to overlook some act and thereby excuse it.
19. impending—imminent; approaching.
20. diligent—painstaking; assiduous; industrious.
21. tenacity—persistency; cohesiveness; holding fast.
22. stipulate—to bargain; to arrange definitely; to specify.
23. articulate—distinct speech; spoken intelligibly.
24. orifice—aperture; an opening.
25. empathy—feeling what someone else feels.
26. ludicrous—incongruity; foolish; ridiculous.
27. enmity—hostility; ill will; antipathy.
28. esoteric—private; understood by only those involved; belonging to one special group.
29. vociferous—loud; clamorous; blatant; boisterous.
30. pusillanimous—cowardly; lacking courage; weak-minded.
31. parsimonious—penurious; stingy; excessively frugal.
32. acrimonious—caustic; harsh or biting tongue.
33. superfluous—surplus; wasteful; extravagant.
34. surreptitious—done stealthily; clandestine; done in a sneaky manner.

A Test of Abstract Intelligence

Instructions: Select the item in each series that does not belong with the other three. For example, in the series, cat, dog, mouse, apple—apple does not belong because it is a fruit while the others are all animals. After you have made your selections *and listed your reasons for your selections,* check the answers and scoring that follow the test.

1. 2, 8, 7, 4

2. baseball, golf, basketball, football

3. Chan, Sawyer, Hardy, Holmes

4. president, chief justice, senator, governor

5. 36, 72, 121, 144

6. father, son, mother, child

7. indifference, love, hate, concern

8. slice, hook, curve, top

9. potato, carrot, squash, onion

10. 9, 7, 4, 8

11. Harold, Sam, Remus, Tom

12. whale, man, bass, porpoise

13. heterosexual, bisexual, asexual, homosexual

14. tomato, pea, corn, lettuce

15. peanut, almond, macadamia, cashew

16. good, justice, evil, law

17. axial, radial, distal, proxial

18. limestone, shale, sandstone, marble

19. white dwarf, red dwarf, sun, moon

20. isostatic, fault, complaint, fissure

Answers:
1. 7—the only odd number.
2. football—use of a non-round ball.
3. Sawyer—the rest are famous detectives.
4. chief justice—the only one not elected.
5. 72—a non-perfect square number.
6. child—the others all denote a gender.
7. indifference—the others all show some involvement.
8. curve—the rest pertain to golf language.
9. squash—it alone grows on top of the ground.
10. 8—the only symmetrical number.
11. Harold—the others are famous "Uncles."
12. bass—the others all swim but are mammals.
13. asexual—the only one not sexual in some manner.
14. tomato—the only one that is a fruit.

15. peanut—this one is not a nut; it is a legume.
16. law—this is an act, not an abstraction.
17. distal—the others imply some connection to the center.
18. marble—the others are sedimentary rocks; marble is a metamorphic rock.
19. moon—the others all relate to a sun.
20. complaint—the others are conditions of the earth's layers.

Scoring: Credit one point for a correct answer and three points for correct answer *and* correct reasoning.

Ratings:

55-60	very gifted
49-54	very superior
42-48	superior
36-41	above average
29-35	high average
25-28	average
19-24	low average
15-18	below average
14 and under	poor

The Proverb Test

Instructions: Write the best explanation you can think of for each of the following. Then score your responses according to the answers provided at the conclusion of the test. You then can rate your performance according to the scale provided.

Proverbs

1. Don't make mountains out of mole hills.

2. Don't count your chickens before they hatch.

3. A bird in the hand is worth two in the bush.

4. The squeaky wheel gets the oil.

5. It's never the tigers that get you, it's the gnats.

6. A rolling stone gathers no moss.

7. A stitch in time saves nine.

8. Don't hang dirty linen out in public.

9. A wise fish never swims upstream.

10. It takes two to tango.

11. Empty wagons make the most noise.

12. People who lives in glass houses shouldn't throw stones.

13. We forget our joys quicker than our sorrows.

14. Four walls do not a prison make.

15. Big trees little acorns make.

16. You can't judge a book by its cover.

17. Rome wasn't built in a day, but they got a good start.

18. He who fights and runs away lives to fight another day.

19. Don't be a pot that calls the kettle black.

20. If you can't stand the heat get out of the kitchen.

Answers: Proverbs are difficult to score because they are abstractions that tell us something about life. A generalized meaning has been provided for each proverb. You must use your best judgment to determine whether you have captured the essence of the meaning of each proverb. If you feel that your meaning is essentially the same as that provided, credit yourself with two points. If you have a portion of the meaning, score one point in your favor. A rating scale is given after the answers.

1. Don't make too much out of something. Don't exaggerate or overemphasize, especially something negative.

2. Don't assume that you have something until you actually do. Don't assume you have an accomplishment until you have it.

3. It is better to have something—to have it in reality—than it is to have something only in theory that is perhaps greater or better.

4. Those who demand the most get the most attention. You have to call attention to your situation in order to get something.

5. It's the little things that trap us, not the big ones.

6. A person who keeps moving will not gain encumbrances.

7. If you attend to something at the right time you will save much time later. Do it now and you save more work later.

8. Don't discuss your problems in public.

9. Don't do things the hard way—go with the natural flow of life and reduce your efforts.

10. One person alone can't accomplish much either negatively or positively: you can't fight or get into trouble alone.

11. Those with little depth are those most ready with empty talk and meaningless chatter. The deep person is more reserved.

12. Those who are vulnerable should not criticize others.

13. Mankind dwells on the bad and neglects the good.

14. Restrictions exist in the mind.

15. Big things often have very small beginnings.

16. You should not generalize or draw conclusions based only upon outward appearances.

17. It takes time to accomplish great deeds, but one first must make a start.

18. Discretion is the better part of valor. It is better to walk away from imprudent risks.

19. Those who have faults should not criticize others who have similar faults.

20. If you can't stand pressure and criticism don't place yourself in a position where you will receive such. Those who are sensitive should not be in a challenging situation.

Analyzing Your Performance

Points	Rating
35-40	gifted
30-34	very superior
27-29	superior
23-26	above average
20-22	high average
18-19	average
15-17	below average
13-14	well below average
12 and under	very poor

The Creative Intelligence Test

Instructions: Each of the following problems has a rather simple solution. To solve the problem you must look to the unusual; a conventional approach simply won't work. Use not only your intelligence but your creativity as well. Then check the answers at the conclusion of the test.

1. Arrange ten dots so that there are four in each row and a total of five rows.

2. Below are nine circles. Your task is to draw four straight lines through all nine circles. You are not allowed to: a. lift your pencil from the paper; b. pass through any circle twice; or, c. retrace any line. You may cross one line one time only.

O   O   O

O   O   O

O   O   O

3. You wish to pour exactly thirteen gallons of water into a barrel. However, you have only a five- and a six-gallon can. How can that be done?

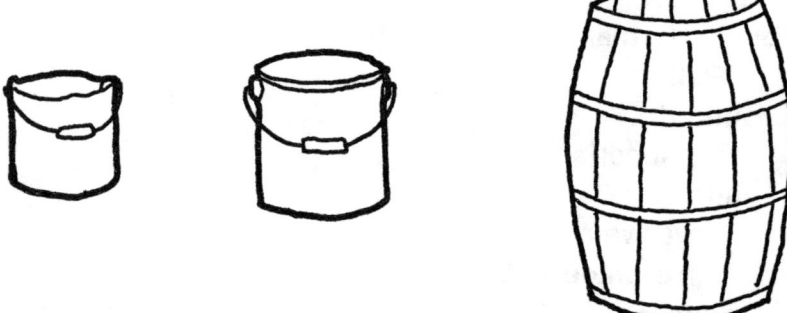

4. You have nine bags of coins. One bag is either too light or too heavy. You wish to identify which bag it is but you only have a balance scale. Can you do it in four tries?

5. Here are five coins arranged in the shape of a cross. However, the cross is lopsided. You are allowed to move only one coin one time. Make your move to even the cross. There are two ways that this can be done. Try to find both:

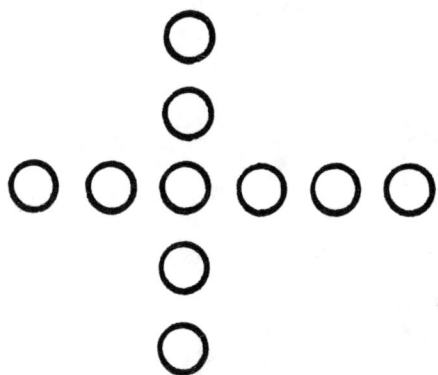

6. Below are sections of a chain. You wish to connect these sections so that you have one circular chain with all links fastened together. To make a circular chain, you will need to cut and then close links, but you wish to do so with the fewest cuts. This can be accomplished with only four cuts. Can you figure out how?

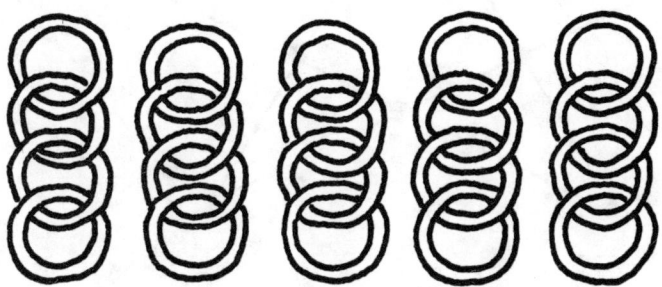

7. Using the six sticks pictured below, arrange them so that you have four equilateral triangles.

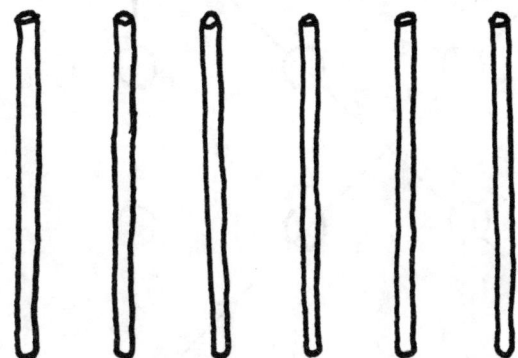

8. Joe was asked to deliver a box containing nine donuts. The donut maker marked the box with Roman numerals IX to indicate the contents. On the way, Joe realized he was hungry. Temptation won out and he ate three donuts. To cover up, he decided to change the markings on the box, but he discovered that his pencil had no eraser. His boss was perfectionistic and never would cross out numbers. Joe figured out a way to alter the numbers without crossing out and without being able to erase. Can you?

Solutions:

1.

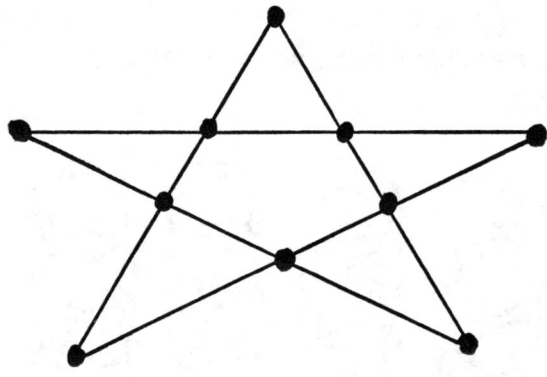

2.

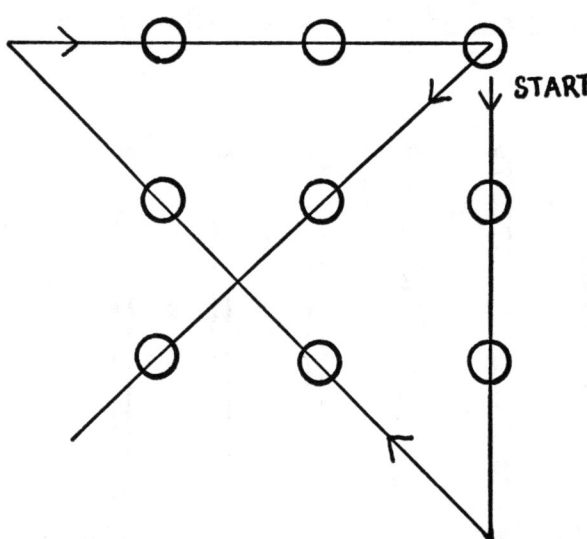

3. Fill the barrel twice with the six-gallon can. Then refill the six-gallon can, pour five gallons into the five-gallon can, and pour the one gallon remaining in the six-gallon can into the barrel.

4. There are four steps to this solution.

    1. If these balance, the irregular bag is among the other three. That would make an easier solution, as we then could go to step #3. Let's assume these don't balance. Then we set bags 1, 2, 3 against 7, 8, 9.

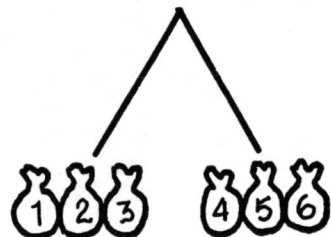

2. Let's assume it doesn't balance. We then know that the good bags are numbers 4, 5, 6, 7, 8, 9.

3. If this balances, the irregular bag is No. 3. Let's assume they do not. Then:

4. We know bag No. 9 is good. If this doesn't balance now No. 1 is the uneven bag. If these do balance the uneven bag is No. 2.

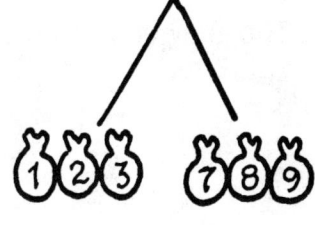
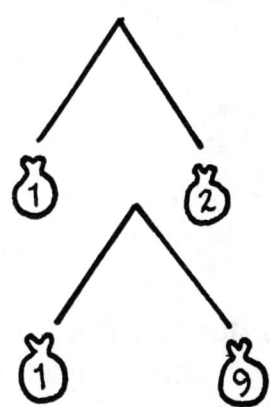

5. There are two moves that can be made.
   1. Move the uneven coin to the middle of the design.
   2. Move the coin off the table.

6. Cut all the links in that piece of chain that we may arbitrarily call the fifth series. Arrange the others as follows:

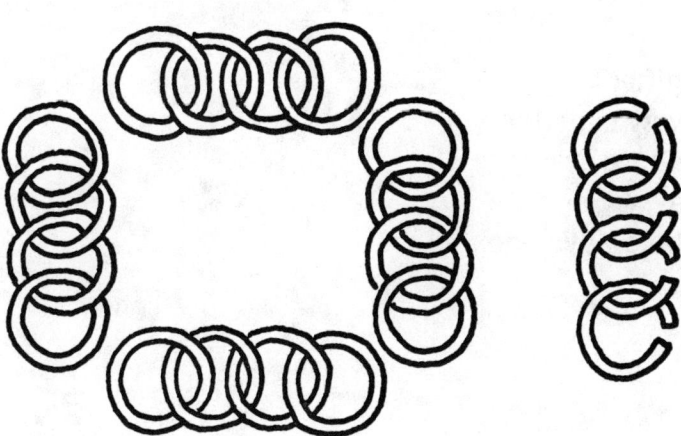

7. The answer is to create a three-dimensional figure, like this:

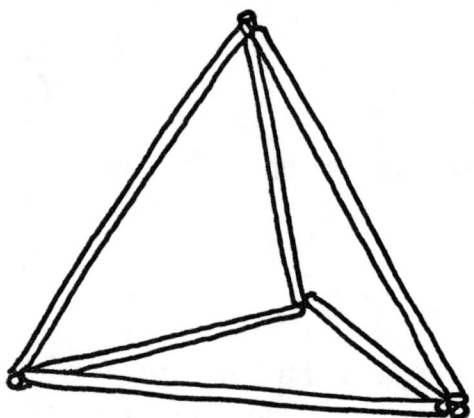

8. Joe was able to find a rather simple answer. The solution lay in adding something rather than in subtracting from the marking. IX therefore becomes SIX.

Score Analysis: These tests are difficult not only because they require intelligent thinking but also because one has to work against existing logic. We all have a set way of looking at things and this set approach is difficult to overcome. There are eight problems, but number five has two answers, each worth one point. Thus, there are nine possible points to be scored in this test.

Ratings
8-9 gifted
6-7 very superior
4-5 above average
2-3 average
0-1 below average

4. Personality Tests

    1. Description Personality Test
    2. Sleep Test
    3. Measurement of Personality Adjustment
    4. The Color Test
    5. The Inkblot Test
    6. Handwriting Analysis

These tests are designed to tell something about the inner you. This is done by making inferences from your behavior. Self-knowledge can be useful if we can learn to accept it without making harsh self-criticisms. People are all to some extent different. That is what makes us interesting—and so very individual.

Description Personality Test

Not all tests of personality are long or complicated. An excellent example of a short, simple, and amazingly revealing test is the Description Personality Test. It can be self-administered and self-scored, as well as given to friends.

This long has been one of my favorite tests because it so interestingly bridges the gap between the professional psychologist and the untrained person. When you master its techniques you will find that it is an enjoyable test to use with friends and at parties—a great ice-breaker. Even the untrained person quickly can become skillful with it.

The results tell much about how others perceive you—whether, for example, you come across as open, warm, available or guarded and reserved. The test reveals basic personality traits but also encourages people to talk about their likes and dislikes. For example, you may find out, as one friend of mine did, that you are motivated more by material things than by dependency on others. This came as a surprise to my friend, because she had always seen herself as extremely tied to other people.

The directions and the analysis of the test data are simple. The main point, though, is to be sure that you obtain sufficiently long answers to the questions to enable you to analyze correctly the individual's personality. Be sure that you understand the directions before you look up the answers on the following pages.

The test consists of only three parts, describing a vase, a flower garden and a key.

I. Vase

Describe your ideal vase.

This is the most important point, the description of the vase. Is it opaque, translucent? Is the vase ornate or plain?

Tell what you'd most like to put into the vase. Be sure to spell this out completely.

II. Flower Garden

Describe your ideal flower garden.

What do you put into it?

How is it arranged?

What sort of border have you provided?

III. Key

Describe your ideal key.

What does it open?

The test is just that simple. Now read on for an analysis of the results.

ANALYSIS

I. Vase—The description of the vase represents the SELF.

Highly ornate: The individual who spends a great deal of time describing a highly ornate vase is likely to do the same with himself or herself. Narcissistic involvement is likely with the person who decorates the vase lavishly, but two factors are important.

1. Women tend to be more narcissistic than men because they learn from an early age that to be noticed they must pay attention to their appearance. However, in today's society men are becoming more involved with their appearance. There may be some question as to what this means.

2. This brings us to the second principle. Narcissism does not mean self-love. Quite the opposite. It is more likely to mean self-concern. If the

individual spends a large amount of time on the ornate qualities of the vase, he or she is likely to be self-concerned and to have self doubts.

Often, these people will give excessive time to the proportions of the vase and, in so doing, they are likely to tell what concerns them about their physiques. For example, those who feel they are too heavy stress a tall, thin or slender vase. Those who feel they are too thin widen their vase.

Sides or wall of vase—represent the person's DEFENSES. Another important quality of the vase is its opaqueness or translucency. Those who are overinvolved with ornateness almost never choose a clear vase. They do not wish to have people see into them.

Those who choose opaque sides, for example, have strong defenses, and they do not wish others to see into them. They are apt not to trust others, to feel sensitive and easily hurt. What is even more important is that they do not trust themselves; usually they are ashamed of their emotional impulses.

Contents of vase—tell about the individual's intimate or closest human relations.

An empty vase suggests loneliness, self-doubt and preoccupation.

A growing plant means that a deep and growing relationship is desired.

A number of cut flowers suggests a desire for a number of close but static relationships. Generally, this individual does not welcome change in close human relationships, and there is apt to be friction when intimates do change.

II. **Flower Garden**—indicates the desired variety of close friends.

All of one kind of flowers: The individual is likely to desire only one type of close friend.

How do the flowers grow? The manner in which the flowers are growing is of equal importance. Some people want them all arranged in neat little rows, and indeed this reflects a desire for rigidity with friends. If the flowers grow naturally in the garden, then friends also may be spontaneous and natural.

Border placement: A hedge is symbolic separation from friends; the higher the hedge the greater the separation.

III. **Key**—is symbolic of that which is most prized in life.

Ornate: If the key is highly ornate, it suggests someone who is materially-oriented. The door holds the treasure; it may be to a veritable treasure chest.

Car Key: When the visualized key is that to a car, the car itself must be analyzed:
- Does it represent wealth? (luxury car)
- Does it represent excitement? (sports car)
- Does it represent family or interpersonal activities? (camper)

Conclusions: When you've analyzed all of the answers, build a profile to see what has been revealed about your personality. There are some key questions that should be answered. What kind of relationships do you prefer? How can you alter your behavior so that you can attain these relationships? What would you like to have that you don't now have? Do you find that your privacy is invaded? Sometimes it helps to take stock of our lives and determine whether we are finding the social gratification we want.

You also will find that The Description Personality Test easily can be taught to others. Try it at a party, with a date, or with your spouse.

The Sleep Test

There are a number of reasons why sleeping can be considered one of the most fascinating of all human activities. It is a natural activity and, to a great extent, free of psychological defenses. Psychological disturbances often show up during sleep and may determine our emotional make-up for the following day. Any number of patients have told me, "I am more tired in the morning than I was when I went to bed." Others report that sleeping is a creative process and, as such, they awaken with new ideas that solve old problems. This takes place for some because the conscious mind is somewhat suspended. This frees the less logical unconscious mind to develop new concepts.

Patterns of sleep can show a great deal about one's personality. These patterns may reveal a desire for change versus a leaning toward what is known. This is important because we might be fighting an inner battle that consumes much of our inner vitality. Sleep patterns also may reflect upon our need for closeness versus our need for independence.

The fact is that your patterns of sleep can tell a great deal about your personality. Psychologists study behavior in order to understand the individual's basic personality (one-third of human behavior consists of sleeping). To understand what your sleep patterns mean, you will need to first describe objectively your own patterns and then see where they fit into the criteria described below.

Sleep Positions

1. Some persons primarily sleep on their backs. These individuals generally face problems in an open and direct manner. They relate logically in human relationships, they are trusting but not gullible, and have a firm grip upon reality.

2. Many persons sleep for the greater part of the night on their stomachs. These individuals are more guarded than the first type, are less prone toward logical thinking, and in general more inclined to deal with problems by postponement or even avoidance. Usually, they are rich in fantasy life. There are some individuals who not only sleep on their stomachs but in addition curl up into a ball. They usually draw their legs up toward their chests. This indicates a desire for affection and closeness with others. These individuals generally have much personal warmth which allows them to relate warmth to others. A drawback is that they may be demanding people who can become overly dependent upon others. They run the risk of being too easily influenced by others. In addition, these individuals often feel rejected when others show some disapproval of their behavior. There are apt to be rather wide ups and downs in their self-concepts. Obviously, this can cause some inner discomfort.

3. A lesser number of people sleep on their sides. Generally, they roll around more at night, which suggests restlessness and worry. These individuals would like to be more open with friends than they are. They vacillate between guardedness and openness. They do not as a rule forget their problems when they go to bed.

Sleep Intensity

All statements obviously are generalizations and, as such, they will not fit each individual. Usually, though, persons who are light sleepers are on guard. They hear all noises and are easily awakened. Once awake, they worry about their inability to sleep. When they do not immediately fall asleep, they worry about their health.

The heavy sleeper often is described as a person who could sleep through a bomb blast. Sleep to these individuals often is an escape. They may take problems to bed with them, but once there, all is forgotten. They may not be obsessive about problems and usually will tend to put off solving them. The hope is that these problems somehow will take care of themselves, and often they do.

Sleep Duration

Eight hours of sleep is adequate for nearly everyone, but it is not uncommon to require only seven hours of sleep. Persons who sleep less than six hours a day are likely to either 1. nap for brief periods during the day; 2. have enormous energy levels; 3. and/or be very relaxed people. However, a very high energy level also may mean a high-strung personality. Anxiety is likely in this case, but not depression. Generally, nervous persons gradually wear themselves out and then go on short sleep binges. Relaxed persons are apt to be consistent and to need less sleep. Emotional tension generally takes a toll and will not allow people to go indefinitely at a fast pace. Relaxed persons restore themselves easily with less sleep because demands upon their energy systems are of lower intensity.

Individuals who require great quantities of sleep (more than nine hours per night) are likely to be depressed. They move at a slower pace, may awaken tired and become quickly run down. Life is quite literally overwhelming and discouragement is a constant companion.

Dreams

It has been said that everyone dreams every time he or she sleeps. Many people are unaware of that fact. As a rule, these people are more emotionally repressed and less able to face up to their conflicts. They often lack emotional spontaneity and tend to avoid their conflicts. Nevertheless, they do go on functioning and keep themselves on an even keel. They may lack flexibility, but generally they are stable.

People who have bad dreams are most often fearful of something that they can't face. They show themselves to be fearful, but their anxiety is non-specific and they can't quite get at the core of their conflicts. They usually are on the dependent side in relating to others and are afraid to try new things on their own.

Individuals who remember most of their dreams and experience many pleasant dreams are very creative. Often, their problems seem to solve themselves. They are marked by traits of flexibility, spontaneity, warmth, constant emotional growth, and the ability to face up to life's problems. They usually are self-analytical and more open in communicating to others things that disturb them.

These are the patterns of sleep. To determine where you fit, sit down and summarize your sleep pattern for one week. You might even ask your spouse to help you describe it. When you have summarized your own pattern, apply the analysis. You should find that it tells a great deal about your personality. That may help pinpoint attributes you wish to strengthen and conflicts you desire to erase. It is likely that you will experience some surprise at what is revealed. A word of caution: There are fluctuations in sleep patterns, so that almost no one finds that these patterns are perfectly constant. You must select for analysis that pattern that is most typical.

However, fluctuations in sleep pattern may be very significant. For example, my wife and co-author, Vi, is able to determine when I am wrestling with a problem. This has happened even when I am unaware of the conflict and usually, with her clues, I am able to resolve it. Others have reported finding in fluctuations of sleep patterns clues as to when they needed a change in their lives.

Measurement of Personal Adjustment

Introduction: How well adjusted am I? What thinking person has not asked himself or herself that question at one time or another? Today, everyone worries, but at what level of intensity does worrying indicate a significant disturbance? Each person needs and generally desires some time alone, but at what point do we become withdrawn? Everyone experiences angry feelings each day, but what makes anger excessive? Some fun is indicative of a sound emotional adjustment, but how much pleasure-seeking is needed to show good adjustment?

We all recognize that we have problems, but we need to have some sort of yardstick to measure when we need extra help. This test seeks to answer these kinds of questions, and also serves an additional purpose. After you complete this test you will also have some insight into the mental health of those close to you. This may help in recognizing when others may need help.

Instructions: To each of the following statements answer "yes" if it applies to you, and "no" if it does not. Then read the scoring procedures at the end of the statements.

1. I have many friends.
2. I have a very fun-filled sex life.
3. I enjoy a deeply intimate sexual relationship.
4. I am a relaxed person.
5. I love physical closeness.
6. I am able to talk out my anger.
7. I take pride in my work.

8. I love physical activity.
9. I am an outgoing person.
10. I enjoy music.
11. I enjoy talking to people.
12. I am very ambitious.
13. I am very competitive.
14. My work is fun to me.
15. I am very refreshed after a few hours of sleep.
16. I generally enjoy good health.
17. I feel good when I know that I look good.
18. Sometimes it is fun to just relax and do nothing.
19. I am generally thought to be easy-going.
20. I have a number of hobbies which give me much enjoyment.
21. There are many little things that give me joy.
22. I have a need to communicate with others.
23. I look forward to sexual activity.
24. I feel that I am adequate at many things.
25. I express my emotions regularly.
26. Our family loves gourmet food.
27. I enjoy an after-dinner drink.
28. I am a very discriminating person.
29. I find that eating is fun.
30. Life often seems worthless.
31. I find myself periodically losing interest in things.
32. I am subject to severe blow-ups.
33. I am rather inhibited emotionally.
34. I seem to push people away from me.
35. I seem to be nervous most of the time.
36. I can't make decisions.

37. I need a drink in order to relax.
38. I am seen as being withdrawn.
39. I have let my appearance go downhill.
40. I would nearly always prefer to be alone.
41. I am unable to get my work done.
42. I can't think for myself.
43. I no longer have much drive.
44. I seem to fight with everyone I am close to.
45. I find myself uncomfortable with members of the opposite sex.
46. I am unable to control my temper.
47. I must admit that I drink heavily.
48. I need alcohol at all social events.
49. I do not trust people.
50. Parties are no fun without drinking.
51. Pain and sex somewhat go together.
52. I always have to be better than my friends.
53. Everyone seems better than I am.
54. I hate people who show off.
55. I am often jealous of both my spouse and my close friends.
56. Many things worry me.
57. I have had problems with ulcers.
58. I find it hard to let my hair down and have fun.
59. My sleep is disturbed by bad dreams.
60. I feel forced to do things I don't like and yet I know there is no real reason for the coercion.
61. People generally hurt my feelings.
62. I get very uneasy when I have to spend time alone.
63. I meticulously watch my diet.
64. Somehow I always wake up tired.

65. My appetite is very poor.

66. Quite frequently I can't sit still.

67. I go on the defensive quickly.

68. I have many little phobias.

69. Without frequent sexual outlet I feel very inadequate and depressed.

70. I have frequent headaches.

71. Others seem to have fun at parties—I do not.

72. I am frequently on edge.

73. I have many digestive problems.

74. I sleep nine hours a day.

75. I have had many hangovers from drinking.

76. My stomach gives me constant problems.

77. I find it difficult to get to sleep.

78. I am prone to guilt feelings.

79. I have periodic skin problems.

80. I feel guilty when I enjoy sex.

81. I find my work very depressing.

82. I constantly worry about my health.

83. My palms usually are sweaty.

84. I am afraid to try new things.

85. I worry greatly about the health of my family.

86. I am a very shy person.

87. I never feel that I look as good as other people do.

88. Strangers make me feel uncomfortable.

89. I frequently overeat.

90. No matter what I accomplish, I never am content.

91. About all I ever do is work.

92. People always seem to take advantage of me.

93. Sex is best when it is risky.

94. I run to the doctor with every little pain.

95. I want to dress better than anyone else.

96. I feel empty without physical closeness.

97. I never feel any concern about my sexual adjustment.

98. I generally need to know from others that I look good.

99. People see me as very rigid.

100. I seem to interrupt a great deal.

Scoring: Mental health is a complicated issue. All of us feel some anxiety, depression, insecurity and general discomfort from time to time. All of us have some areas in which we function irrationally or illogically. No one is perfectly healthy at all times. Part of the pattern for a healthy person is the ability to accept something less than perfect, i.e. to recognize and accept personal shortcomings. When we learn to accept a negative trait, no longer are we upset by little things; we are able to cope. We will not succeed in changing ourselves if we deny everything that we do not like about ourselves.

What, then, are some of the qualities of the healthy person? On the positive side is the ability to have fun, experience joy, relate to others, express feelings in a constructive manner, and be productive. Maturity implies responsibility and appropriate use of one's resources. On the negative side, we might say that healthy persons do not worry excessively (or unreasonably), do not experience severe and disabling anxiety or depression, and do not become withdrawn. We have left out of consideration the very serious illness wherein there are superficial emotions, delusions (false beliefs), hallucinations (unreal sensory experience), and the very severe depressions that reduce a person to a virtually non-functioning state. Anyone suffering from such disorders would do well to get professional help immediately.

In regards to this test, however, the reader quickly should obtain an idea of those areas that indicate emotional disturbance. It goes without saying that such realization will only take place if one is able to answer the questions honestly. It then will be up to the individual to determine an appropriate course of action. Some may seek professional help to live a more full life, to experience joy and relate better. Others may try to do it themselves. But, in any case, each person can set his or her own goals and choose an appropriate course of action.

Scoring Answers: Consistent with what has just been stated, the most healthy answers with their weighted scores are as follows:

Questions 1 through 6 "Yes"	10 points each	Maximum 60
Questions 7 through 25 "Yes"	6 points each	Maximum 114
Questions 26 through 29 "Yes"	4 points each	Maximum 16
Questions 30 through 51 "No"	8 points each	Maximum 176
Questions 52 through 86 "No"	4 points each	Maximum 140
Questions 87 through 100 "No"	2 points each	Maximum 28
		Total Possible Points 534

Analysis by Scores

500-534	Excellent Adjustment
475-499	Well Adjusted
425-498	Average Adjustment
375-424	Below Average Adjustment
325-374	Far Below Average Adjustment
324 and below	Poorly Adjusted

Additional Comments: A psychologist cannot leave this test without a few passing words. A score alone is insufficient to appraise so delicate a matter as emotional adjustment. A "yes" answer to questions 30 through 51 is indicative of some significant conflicts no matter what the final total score. To a lesser extent, the same is true of a "yes" answer to questions 52 through 86. It might be wise to check your answers to these key questions and note weak areas, regardless of your overall score. After so doing, you may conclude that you wish to tackle previously undealt-with conflicts. After all, isn't life too precious to live with only partial fulfillment?

The Color Test

Introduction: Color is everywhere around us and affects our lives far more than we can imagine. Color brings out certain moods and suppresses others; it can bring out specific traits in our personalities. There are some colors that tend to depress, while others produce elation. In addition, by identifying our color preferences for everyday objects, we gain an understanding of what subconsciously we are seeking. Do we want passivity in our bedroom, for example, or more subdued affection and closeness? With our appearance and clothing, do we want to be seen as overtly powerful or more flexible and yielding? Sometimes we inadvertently project an image that we do not wish to show. We may seem boisterous when we would like to appear calm and thoughtful. Knowledge gleaned from this test should provide answers to these and many other questions.

Instructions: To successfully complete this test, the reader must be prepared to use his or her imagination.

First, select your three favorite colors (in order of preference) from the following list:

Red	Orange
Yellow	Pink
Blue	Purple
Brown	Green
White	Black

Second, visualize your most ideal automobile. Try to develop a strong mental image so that you virtually can see the car. Now select your three favorite colors, in order of preference, for your ideal car.

Third, imagine how you would like to appear in your clothes—dressing not for work, nor for others, but selecting purely to satisfy yourself. Which three colors, in order of preference, would you like to emphasize with your clothing?

Fourth, picture the ideal bedroom decor. Again, in order of preference, which three colors would predominate?

Scoring: In order to score the selections, we need to know something about colors and how they relate to personality. They are as follows:

I. Colors

1. **Red**—the most emotional and powerful of the colors. Generally, red is favored by true extroverts, by persons who feel deeply, who show their emotions readily, and who are passionate. Those strongly favoring red are apt to be flamboyant, to enjoy people, and to express freely most of their feelings in a direct manner. They may tend to be impulsive at times.

2. **Blue**—is a tranquil color and, as such, it shows persons who generally are well controlled, careful about what they do, introspective, and slow to give loyalties. Once they do commit themselves they tend to be consistent with their loyalties and stick to their selections.

3. **White**—generally chosen by persons who have a strong degree of meticulousness, especially with regard to cleanliness. Persons favoring white tend to be emotionally controlled and philosophically oriented with low material desires. They generally are conservative in political outlook.

4. **Pink**—the person selecting pink is much more conservative than is the

individual selecting red. Feelings may be deep, but there is a tendency to inhibit the expression of emotion at the very onset of any feeling. There exists a great awareness of atmosphere and that, in turn, affects the expression of emotion. The setting has to be perfect before emotion is expressed and thus there is strong perception as to the needs of others. Deep feeling takes place only when clearly accepted by others.

5. **Green**—those selecting this color are earthy, warm, nature-loving, practical, very giving people. They value the opinions of others, seldom are impulsive, but instead are well balanced. They do express emotion, but always in a temperate manner.

6. **Yellow**—this color denotes a casualness and even excessive cheerfulness. When things go badly for this person, there is a tendency to look for the bright side. There is considerable optimism even in the face of adversity. Emotion is expressed, but generally in a casual, cheerful manner. Anger seldom is expressed directly.

7. **Brown**—while these people are sociable, they also tend to be highly responsible. Hard work is a trademark and use of the color, especially in clothing, frequently denotes tiredness. There are strong ties to responsibility for family and to the institutions with which they are involved.

8. **Orange**—this is a mixture of the red and yellow personality. Emotion is tempered; deep feeling is expressed initially but then is tempered by a casual air. There is a strong affinity for the outdoors.

9. **Purple**—these people push others to have a good time. They often are the comedians in the group; they feel badly if others take a serious view of life. They are extremely outgoing and often exhibitionistic.

10. **Black**—the person making this selection tends toward strong conservatism, is very business-minded, serious about life, and suspicious of frivolity. There is a tendency to view life as a series of sharp contrasts, as, for example, between serious and lazy.

What The Other Selections Tell

II Cars

The car we drive is an extension of our ego. Note whether there is consistency between favorite colors and the colors selected for cars. If not, then the person is trying to project something that he or she wishes to be—is trying to hide something from open view.

III Clothes

The clothing we select reveals the image that we wish to project. A basically quiet, introverted person may want to be noticed by others. So red, purple, or yellow are chosen for clothes. The reverse also may be seen, but compare the differences. Those selecting same or similar colors show consistency between their inner self and social image.

IV Bedrooms

What do you project with your love life? Red, remember, is the passionate color—black indicates a lover of contrasts. Chances are that the person selecting black wants a lover to start making love with elaborate, striking clothes, not without clothes or with plain clothing. Propriety is important— as opposed to the impulsive "red person" or casual "yellow person."

Now pull all of the color selections together and note the comments about corresponding personality traits. There are four categories; mark selections in order of preference for each as follows:

I	II	III	IV
Colors	**Cars**	**Clothes**	**Bedrooms**

1.
2.
3.

Conclusions: Now that you have completed the test, you can see what factors are shown regarding your personality. Surrounding yourself with certain colors also can serve as a ploy to mask or accentuate various personality traits. The reds, for example, may help bring out deeper feelings. Conversely, it may be wise to avoid certain purchases, such as a car, when you are in an atypical mood. You would not like to select a car when you are in a rare down mood that won't appeal to you when you are your normal, happy, buoyant self!

A final word: It might be fun to see how your lover and you balance one another.

The Inkblot Test

To many people, an inkblot test has a highly mysterious aura. The fact that such a test could show something about one's personality seems truly mystical. Others, while curious about this time-honored method of personality analysis, are highly skeptical and seek some sort of rationale for the inkblot methodology.

Leonardo da Vinci stated that whenever someone places paint upon a wall, that person also puts something of himself or herself onto that wall. Perhaps it is similar to stating that we reflect our personalities in nearly everything we do, but especially in our creative endeavors.

Creative processes are, of course, difficult to define. For our purposes, we can state that "creative" means to bring something new into existence. In The Inkblot Test, the word "creative" denotes a process whereby meaningless inkblots are interpreted as resembling something definable as a result of one's imagination. It is literally a process of making something out of nothing. Conversely, if the inkblots were deliberately given structure, made to specifically resemble definite objects, the test would be changed dramatically. Persons taking the test then would find their imaginations stifled. To a greater extent they then would see what others see.

It is that lack of clear definition that makes the inkblots useful. That amorphous characteristic allows—even forces—individuals to attribute some portion of their inner selves to the inkblots. The inner person becomes reflected into the inkblots, according to individual needs. A person then can view his or her world as represented by the inkblots in the way that he or she would like that world to be.

That process allows others to take a glimpse at the world of persons taking the test. By so doing, they can determine how persons taking the test would like to interact with others, what their interests are, how lively are their imaginations, how well they organize their worlds, whether they see the world as friendly or hostile, what are their variety of experiences and thoughts, what dominates their thoughts, what are their general goals, and much more.

In short, the inkblot process allows one to get a look at what motivates an individual. The Inkblot Test can be very significant in helping us to understand ourselves.

Instructions: These inkblots were created by the authors, as was the scoring system. This test is not to be confused with the well-known inkblot test. The administering and scoring procedures are very different in this test.

There are eight inkblots. Look at each in turn in any manner you choose. You may turn the book to study the inkblots from different angles should you so choose. Note what the inkblots look like and *be sure to describe your responses fully*, i.e., note actions and postures if any are present.

Then, check the location charts for the number of the part in which you saw your particular responses. This will enable you to pinpoint your response for easy evaluation. Always be sure that you fully understand what you have seen before you go to the scoring section.

Finally, read the scoring system. This will involve reading the standard responses and classifying your responses according to the procedure outlined.

If you now are sure of the directions, turn to the first inkblot and try to find as many things as you can. This test is not timed.

BLOT I

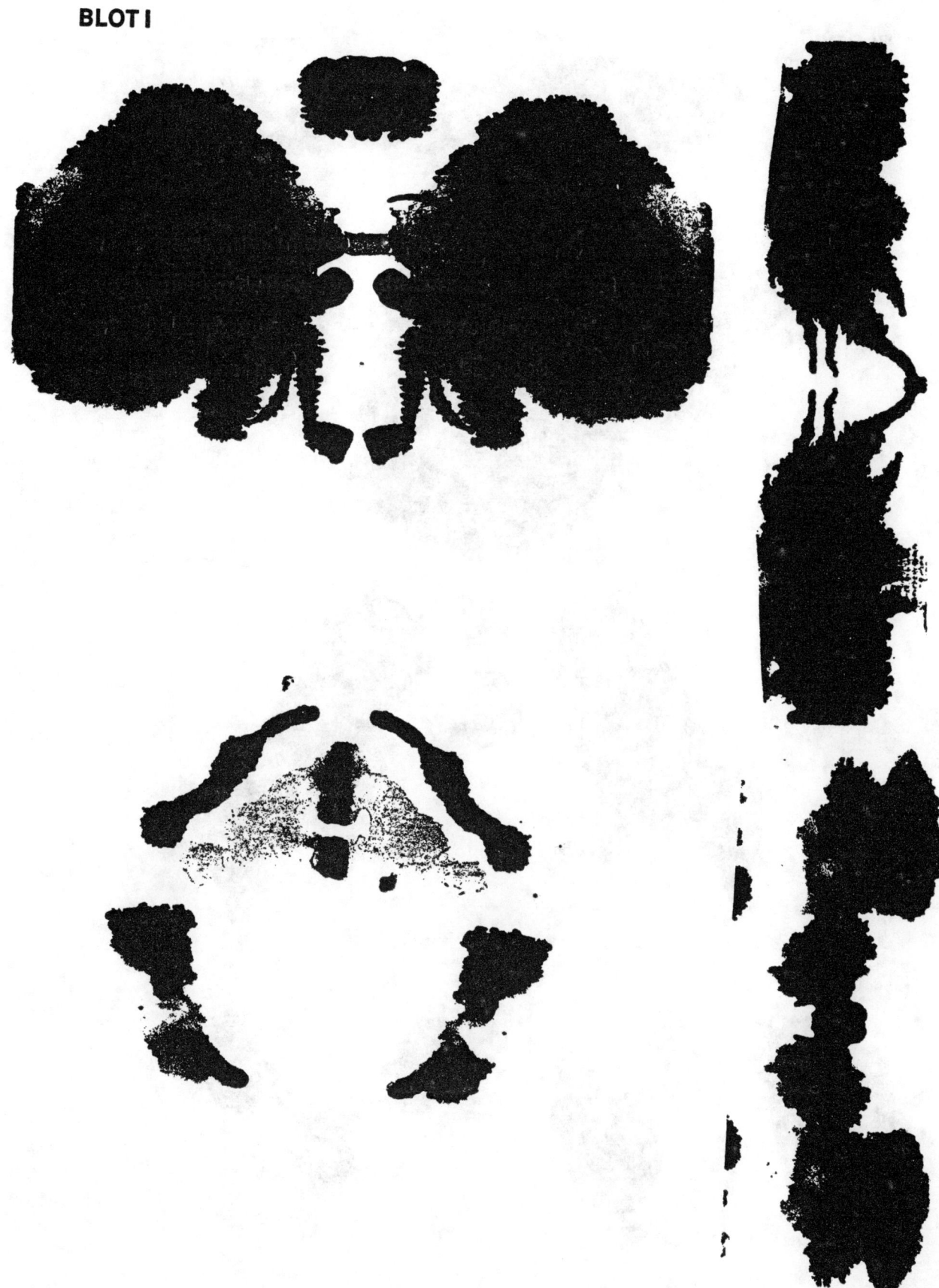

BLOT II

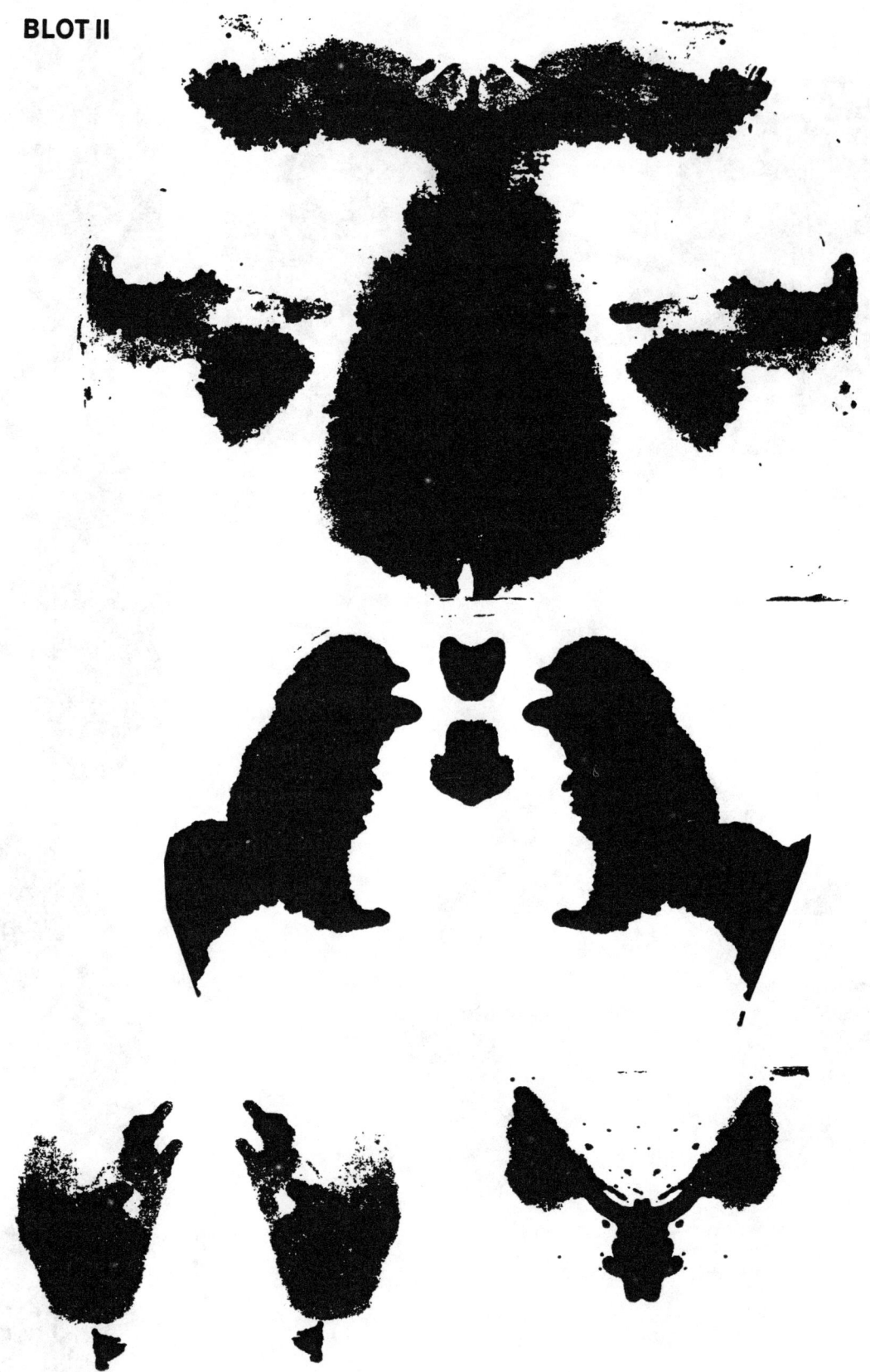

BLOT III

BLOT IV

BLOT V

BLOT VI

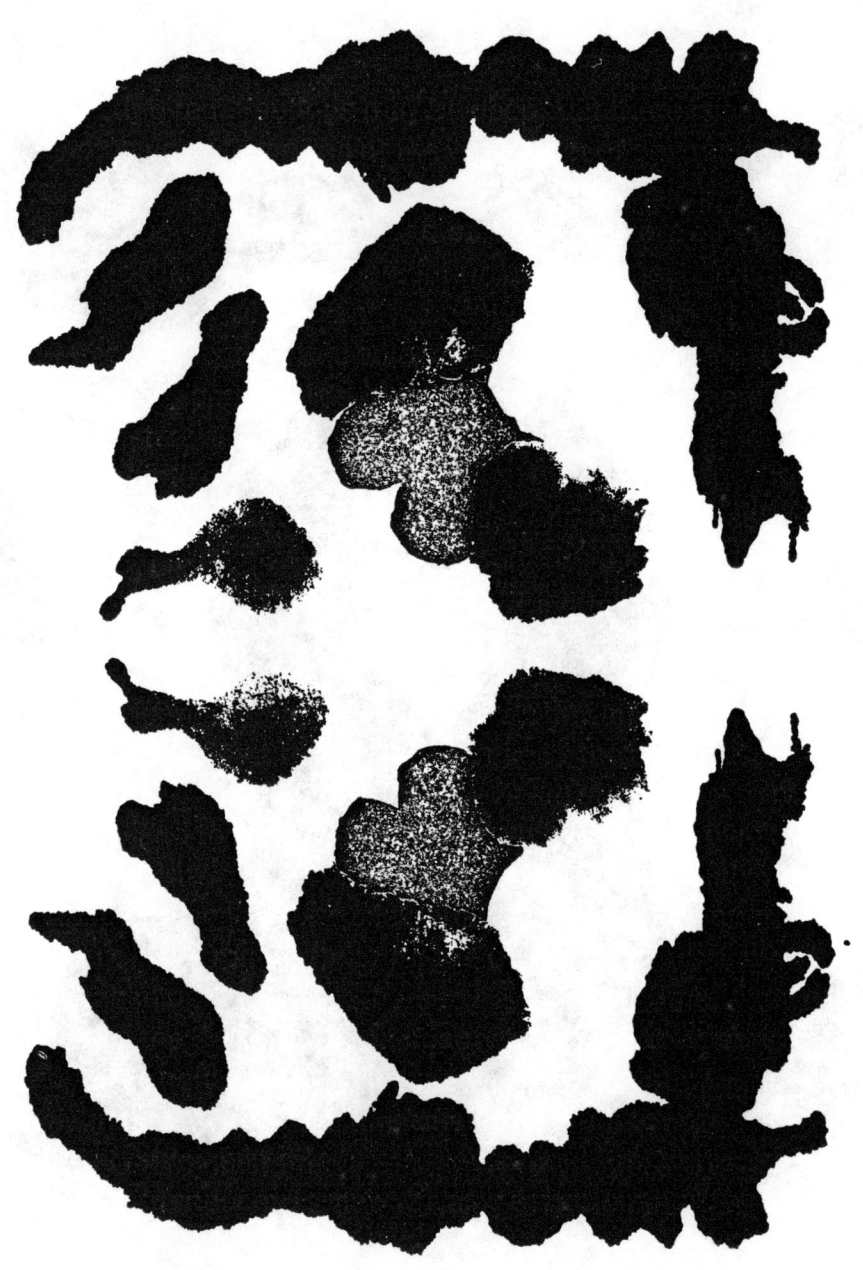

BLOT VII

BLOT VIII

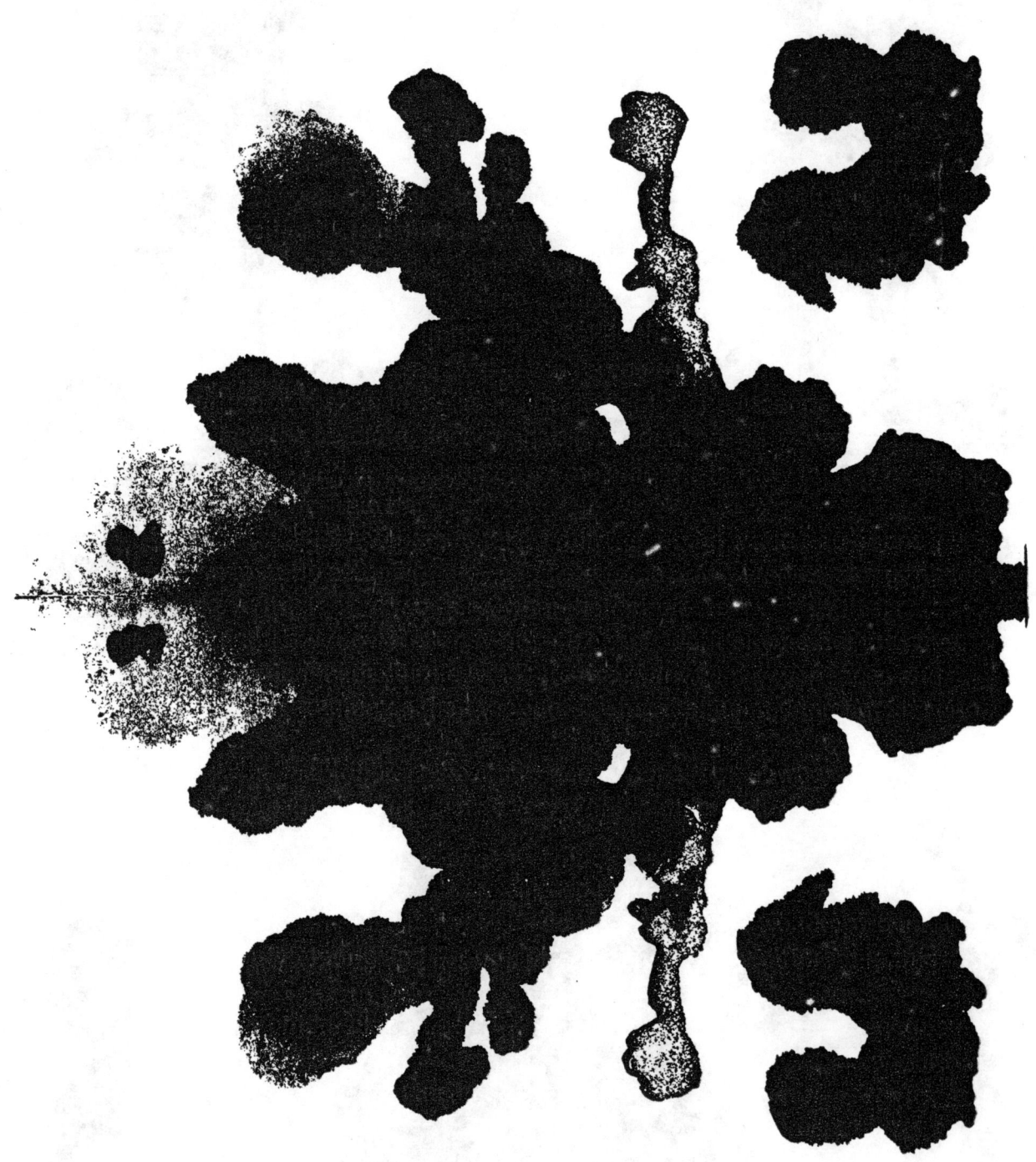

Scoring Instructions: The scoring and analysis of The Inkblot Test undoubtedly is the most complicated in this book. This test requires careful attention to detail in order to produce accurate results.

As an aid to evaluation, we have provided a scoring key to each of the inkblots. Scoring is done in a number of stages. There is a guide to enable you to locate your response by number. A description and classification of responses then is provided for each number. This allows you to evaluate your responses against the responses of the sample groups that first took this test. This will indicated how much or how little your responses resemble those of others.

It is extremely important, however, to recognize that conformity is not a key to evaluating your test performance. We are *not* saying that differences mean abnormality. After all, we are talking here about fantasy rather than a clear perception of reality. Deviation very often means creativity. You will obtain only one measure of personality by noting how similar your responses are to the responses of the test sample. There are a number of scoring categories that must be noted in order to make the test results meaningful. We urge you to read them and then tabulate your performance against an average score. It not only will increase accuracy, but it will provide much more fun. The scoring categories are as follows:

1. **Total number of responses**—provides a means of measuring creative fantasy and flexibility.

2. **Whole responses**—using the entire blot—generally very difficult to see, but this shows high organizational ability.

3. **Small blot areas**—use of the small areas shows close attention to detail.

4. **Procedure**—obtained by noting whether you start with large areas and then progress to the small areas. Working in that direction indicates that you deal with large issues first and then go to the insignificant. If you first tackle small areas of the blots, then a reverse interpretation applies.

5. **Turning the blots**—this show flexibility and adaptability. Those who resist turning the blots dislike change and are overly conventional in their thinking.

6. **Action responses**—perception of people, animals or objects in action. The action may be passive, such as people lying down, or active, such as a rocket blasting off, or people dancing. The greater the number of action responses, the more active the person. The quality of the action tells whether the person is passive or aggressive, or, at least, which they would like to be.

7. **Creative responses**—these are defined as responses not included in the master listings, but of a type that others quickly can see when pointed

out to them. These responses indicate a creative person.

8. **Conventional responses**—this means that one gives primarily those responses that everyone else sees. This would show a degree of conformity but also an ability to share ideas with others.

9. **Type of response**—whether it is animal, human or object. This tells something of our interests. Engineers, for example, see more objects than do psychologists.

10. **Sexual responses**—the fact that they are given shows both interest and ability to talk about this important area of life.

11. **Fearful responses**—e.g., blood, anatomy, weapons, indicate a desire to deal with something that causes discomfort.

These are the major response types—some additional categories are included in the "conclusions" section. After you have checked your responses, set up a table of your responses as compared to the average. You quickly will see your high and low areas and from that will easily obtain a personality profile.

Blot I

Numbering is as nearly clockwise as possible. Maps, rockets, most general objects, and nature responses can be seen nearly everywhere and are not listed. Common responses by the test groups were:

1. Clouds hanging over; people huddled together; a variety of animals; a bomb blast.
2. Animals smoking pipes, fighting or playing; weird people; odd creatures.
3. Face—animal, human.
4.-6. Faces in all areas, human or animal.
7. Elephants—both figures together or separate.
8.-10. Human—faces in nearly all edges of blot.
9. Bat; butterfly; anatomy responses; faces in edges.
11. Birds; sunset; angels.
12. Hand with thumb; faces.
13. Heads; faces.
14. Humans.
15. Heads.
16. Skulls; anatomy.
17. Club; blood smear; people; animals.
18. Statue; art object; temple; monster face.
19. Face, animal or human.
20. Pipe (smoking); club.
21. Faces, human, animals.

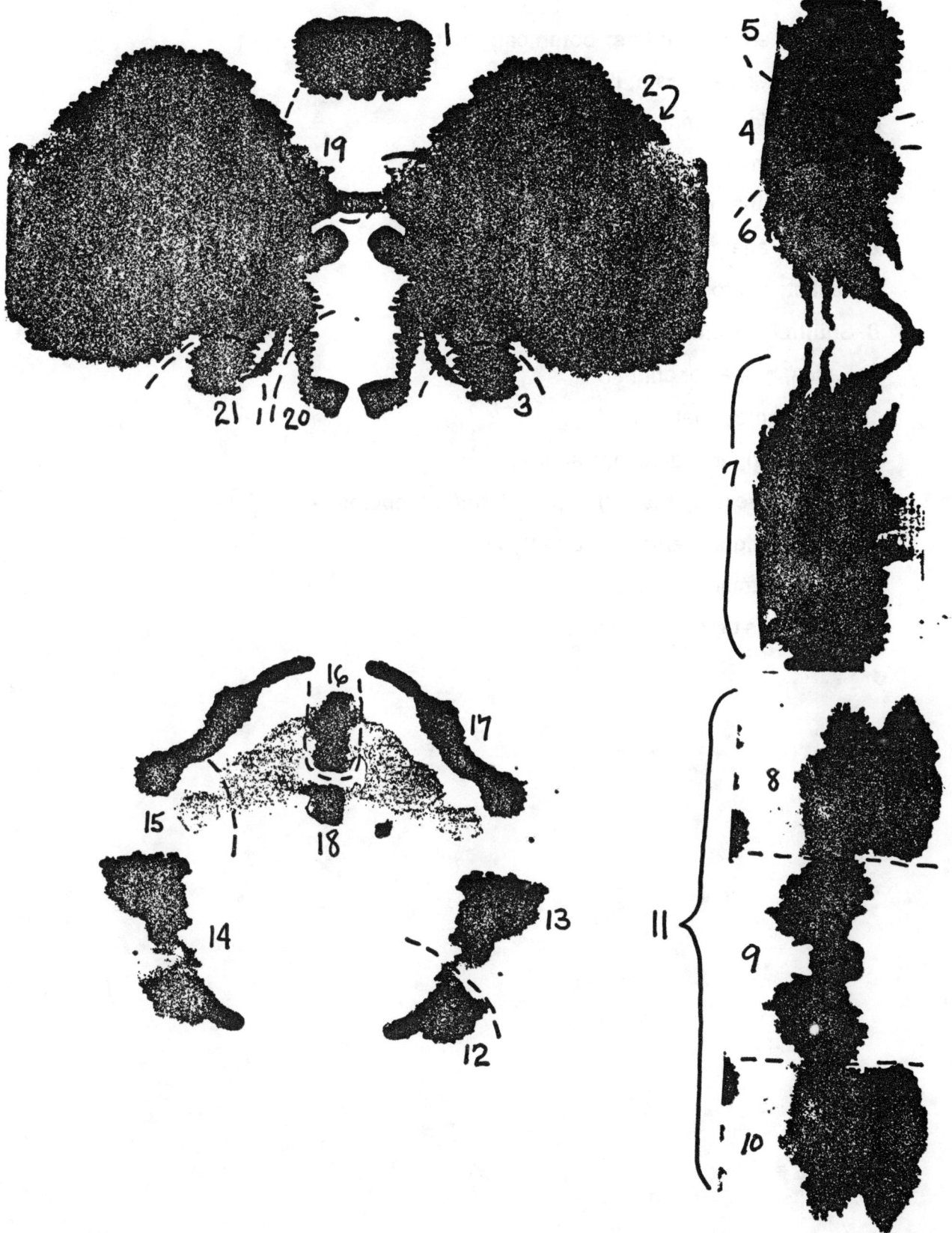

103

Blot II

1. Deer's head and antlers; botanical; anatomy.
2. Animals, chiefly cats, lions; sunsets.
3. Ocean life; animal or plant; anatomy.
4. Face, human or animal.
5. Face, human or animal.
6. Jacket; anatomy; sea shell or stone; animal.
7. Jacket; anatomy; animal.
8. Squirrels; hand puppet.
9. Faces, human or animal.
10. Pompoms; anatomy.
11. Human figure; dancing; anatomy.
12. Female sexual organ; human twisting pompoms.
13. Human figure; animals; bird flying.
14. Face, human, animal.
15. Chickens or fowl; birds.

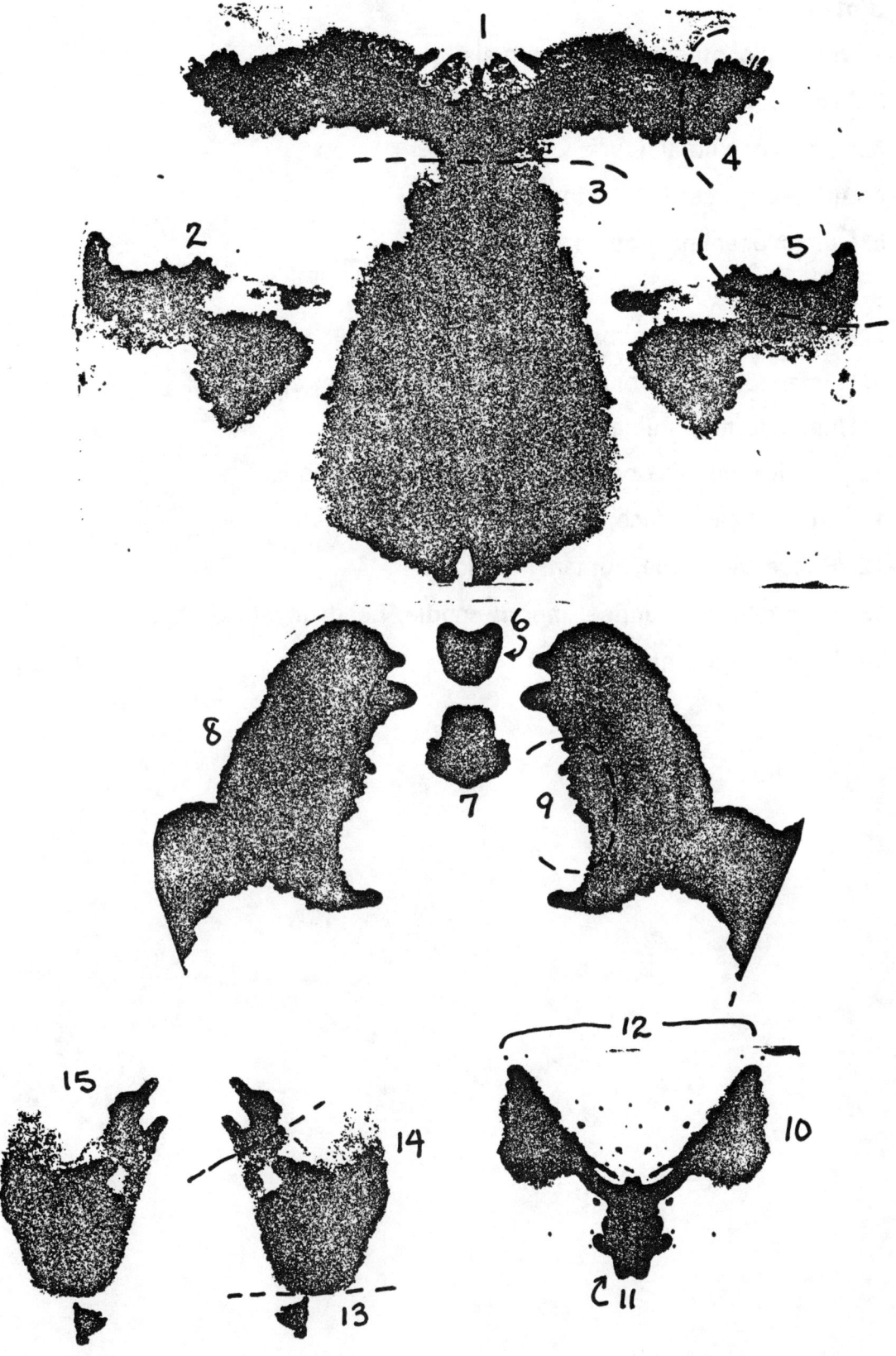

Blot III

1. Dragons or other mythical animals.
2. Faces or heads, human, animal.
3. Human or animal figure.
4. Animal figures; human faces.
5. Human or animal figures.
6. Animal; human heads.
7. Faces, human or animal.
8. Human faces; sun or moon; nature responses; clouds.
9. Human forms; animals; mountain cliffs.
10. Mythical human or animal figures; club (weapons).
11. Animal head or face; weapons; sexual.
12. (Space area) Face, human, mythical.
13. Mountain with sunrise; moon; candle; head; mystical light.
14. Sexual organ; nipple; club.

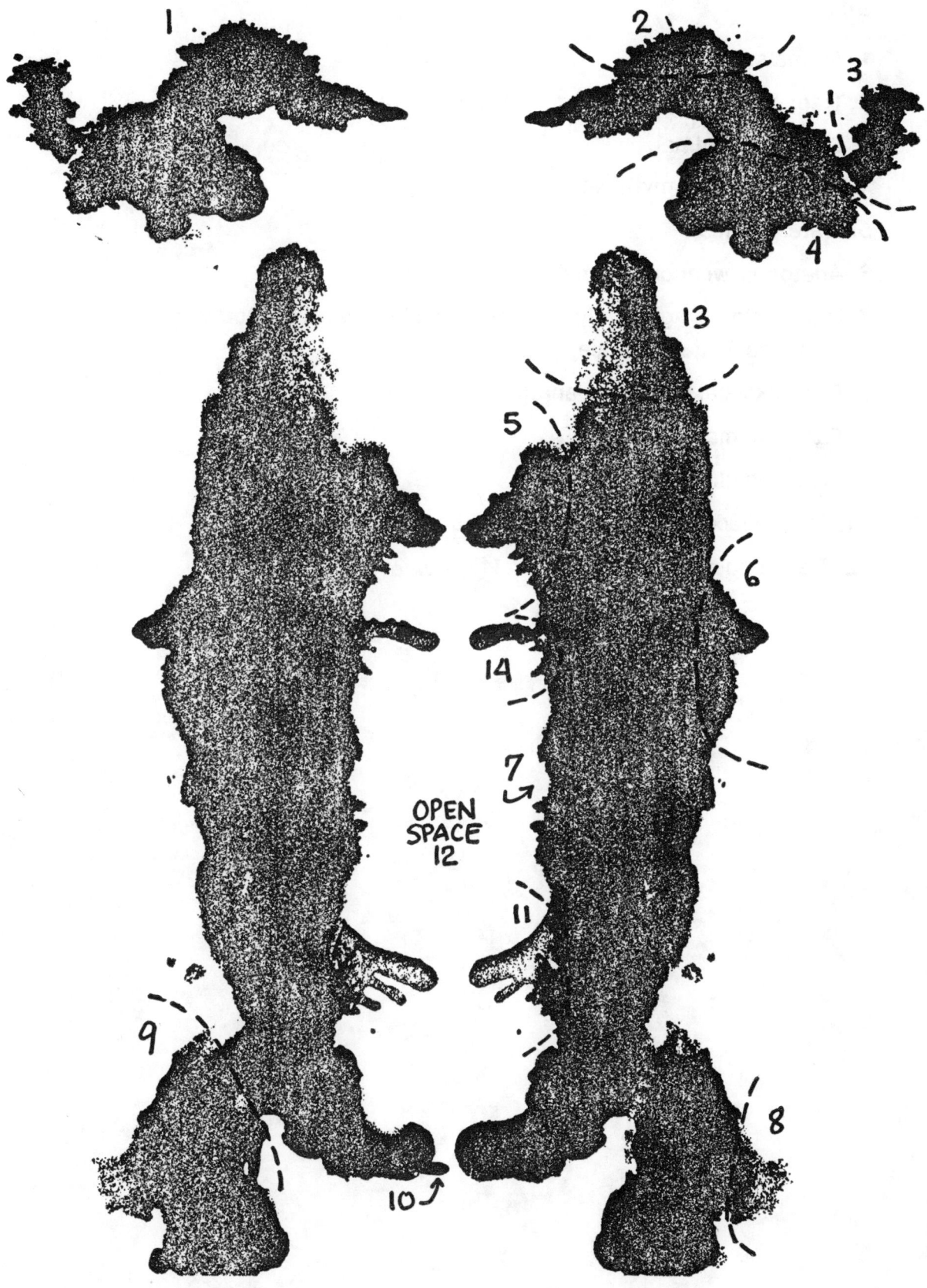

Blot IV

1. Animals.

2. Tree; face—human or animal; sea life; clouds and moon.

3. Seashore; animal.

4. Face, animal or mythical.

5. Water; animal.

6. Anatomy; weapon; animal.

7. Human figure—generally in something like a cave; anatomy; sexual response, usually female; animal.

8. Bird; skeletal response; anatomy.

9. Faces, human, animal.

10 Bird's head.

11. Animal faces; portion of sun; sea shore.

12. Tree; ghost; weapon; mythical figure.

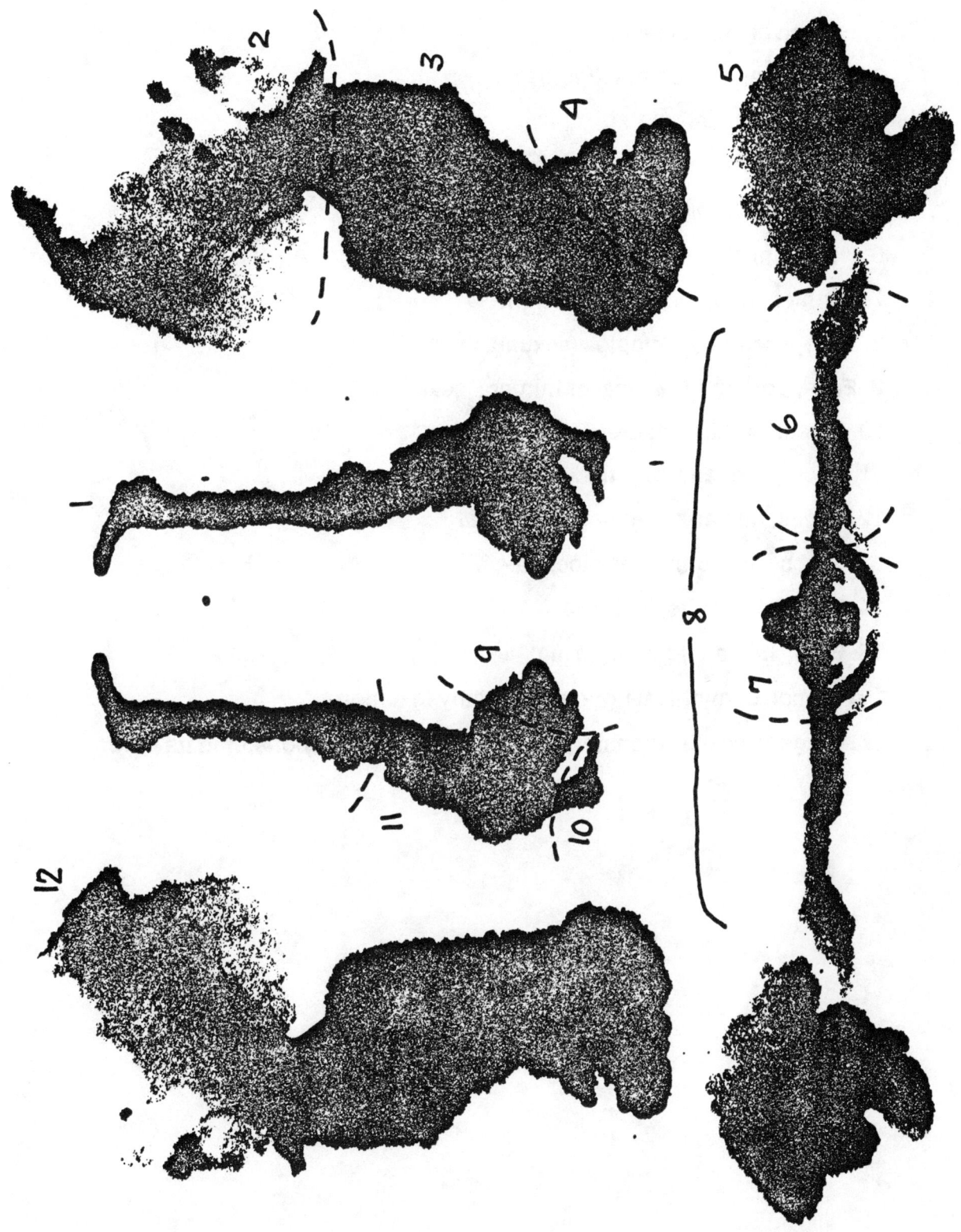

Blot V

1. Human or animal face.
2. Club (weapon); animal figure.
3. Animal; sunset.
4. Face, animal or human.
5. Face, animal or human; mythical figure.
6. Head, animal or human.
7. Mythical figures, often in action.
8. Face, portion of; nipples (sexual).
9. Face, portion of, animal or human; sexual.
10. Trees; huddled figures.
11. Faces, human or animal.
12. Faces, human or animal; weapons.
13. Clubs (weapon); seascape; trees.
14. Mythical figures; humans.
15. Bats; human figures; sexual.
16. Human or mythical figures, generally in action.
17. Dragon; snake; monster; mythical worms; sea monster in its cave.

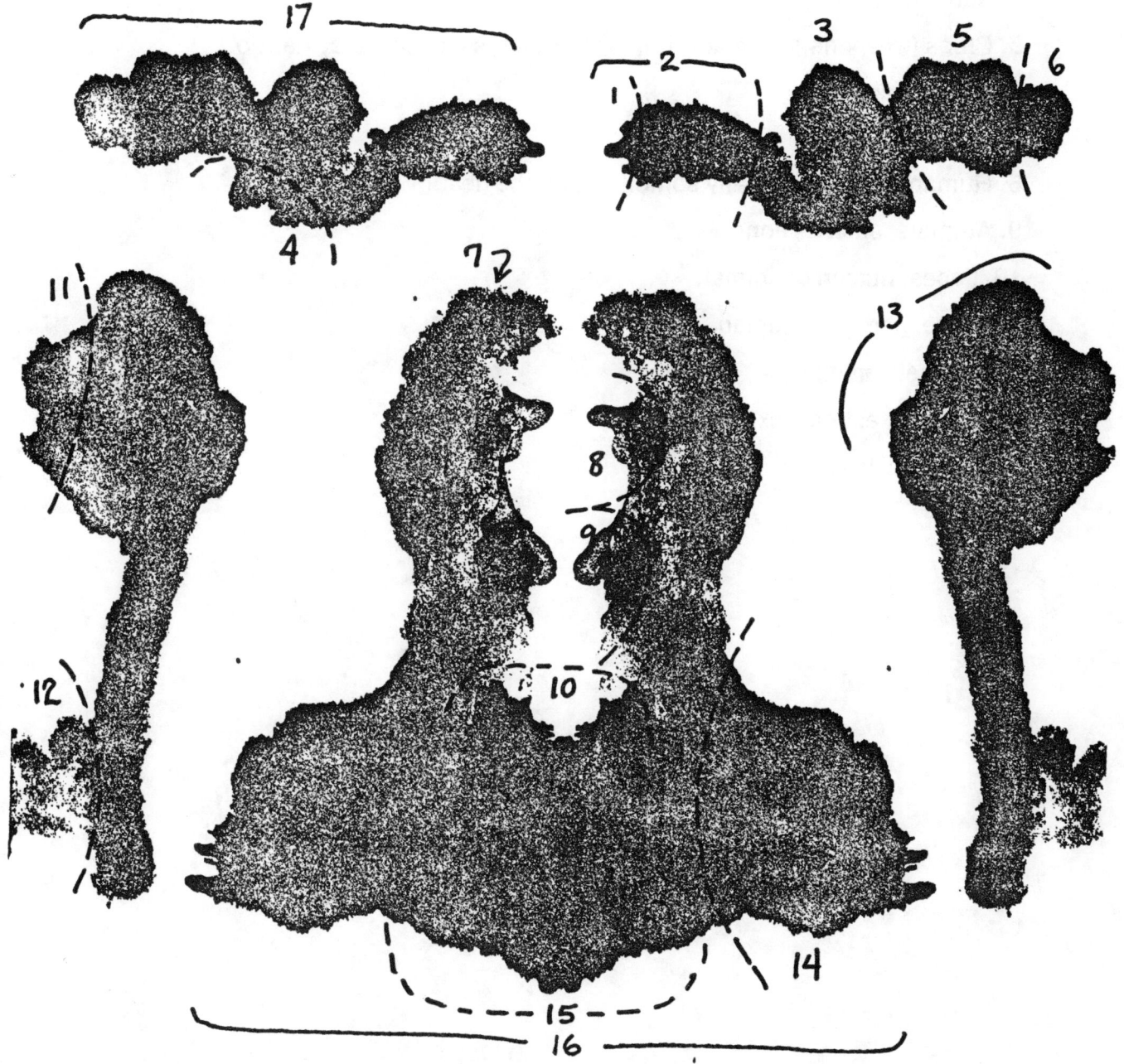

111

Blot VI

1. Duck- or bird-like figures; trees; humans; shoes (top portion).
2. Animal or human figures.
3. Animal figures.
4. Sunset; animal.
5. Clubs (weapons); animals; humans; objects like baskets; hairdo.
6. Human face.
7. Human; tree.
8. Human figure, especially something on the head.
9. Animals, such as lions.
10. Faces, human or animal.
11. Face, generally human.
12. Sunset; animal.
13. Sunset; animal; explosion.
14. Botanical; animal.

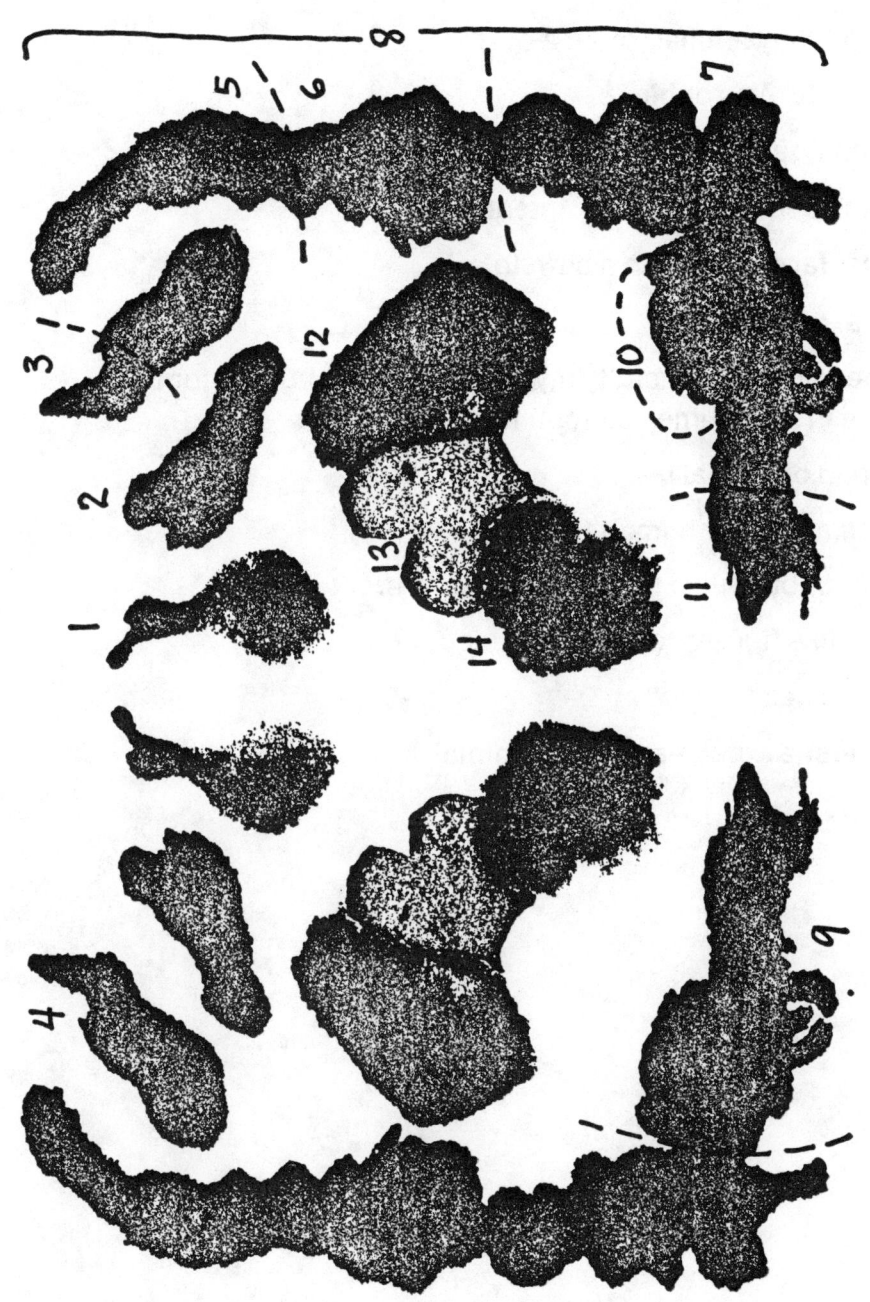

Blot VII

1. Head, animal or human.
2. Face, animal or human.
3. Face, mainly animal, often a bird's.
4. Face, chicken's or bird's.
5. Human figure, child, or mythical; animal.
6. Animal, especially like an anteater.
7. Animal face, often like a buffalo's.
8. Animal or botanical.
9. Winged animal, generally mythical, perhaps human form; person in a costume; cartoon figure.
10. Human or animal head.
11. Small animal or human figure.
12. Face, or botanical form; human figure.
13. Duck-like figures, often embracing.
14. Animal head.
15. Pincers; sexual responses; animal.

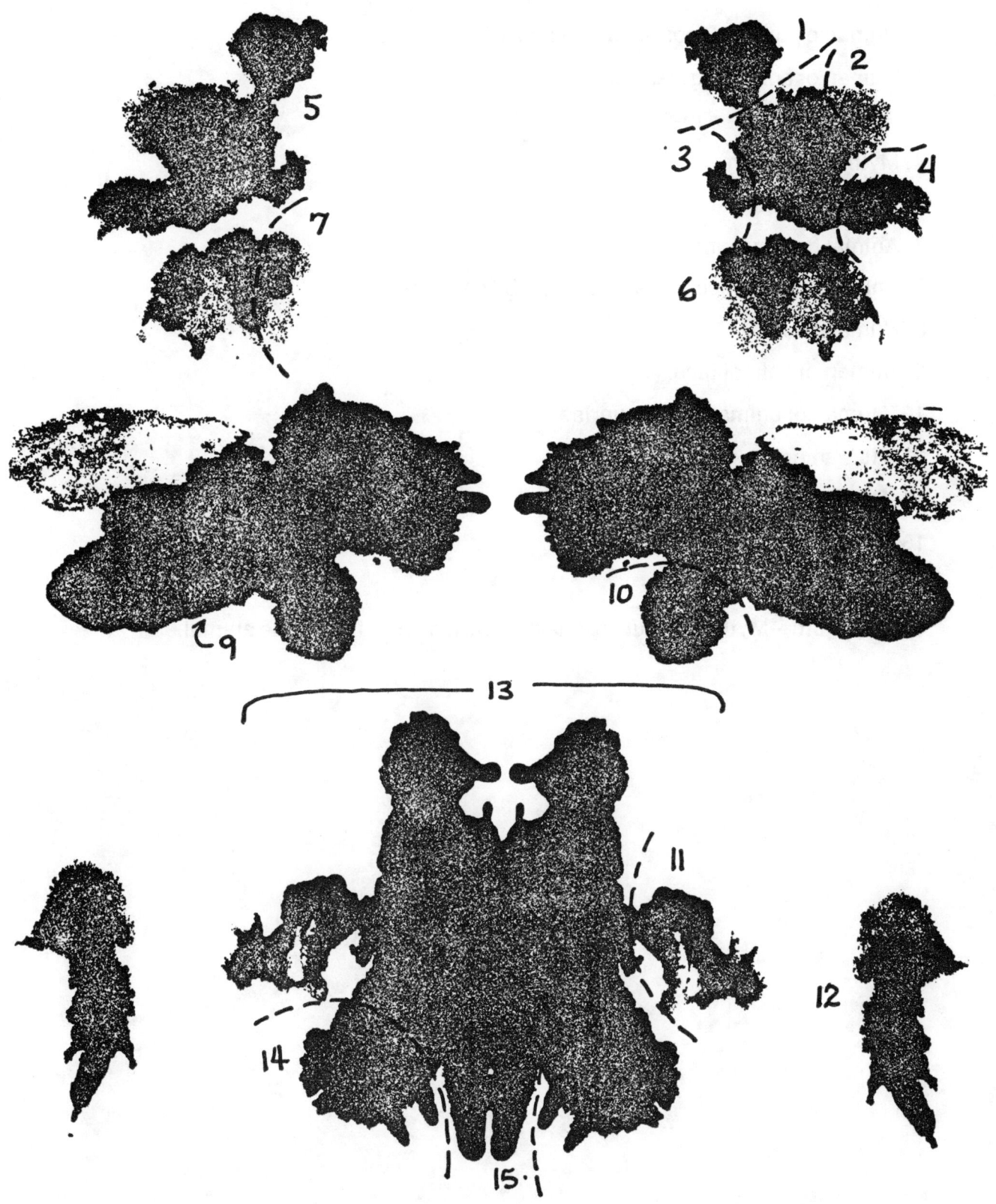

Blot VIII

1. Human or animal face; sexual, usually female; lips.

2. Human or animal figures; embryos; eyes.

3. Face, human or animal.

4. Mythical creature.

5. Wings; animal legs.

6. Animal heads; sunset.

7. Animal head, especially serpent; club (weapon).

8. Human head.

9. Human or animal face.

10. Human or animal head; sunrise.

11. Human figure.

12. Horse-like figure.

13. Human or animal face.

14. Human or animal face.

Whole figure—Mythical figure, arms out, with boys riding some animal.

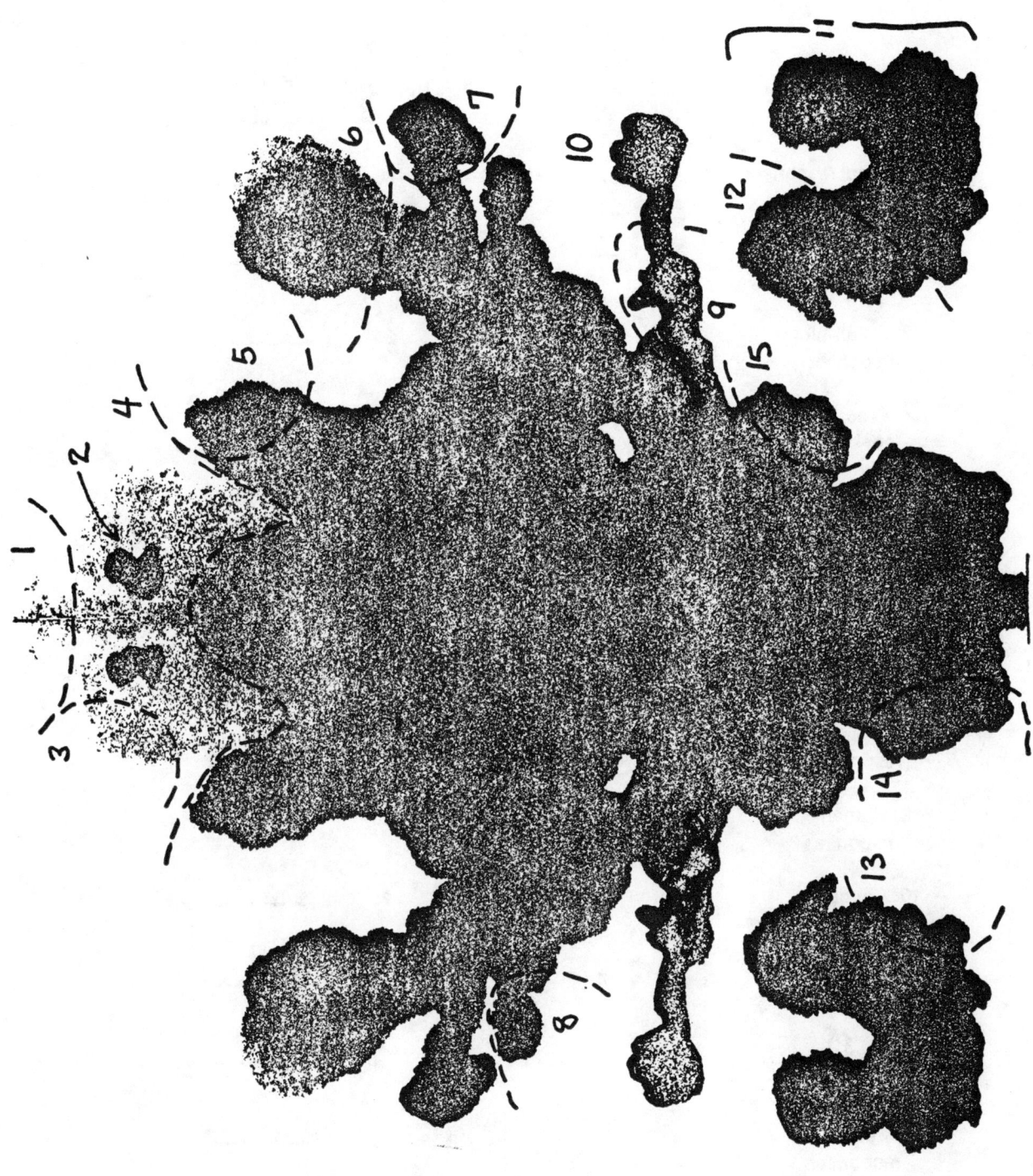

Inkblot Test—Scoring Chart

	Low average	Average	High Average	Very High	Reader's Responses
1. Total responses all blots	32	40	48	56	_____
2. Total-blot responses	0	0	1	2	_____
3. Small-blot responses	10	18	25	30	_____
4. Procedure—Average (per blot)	3 small 1 large	2 small 1 large	3 small 3 small	6 large 4 small	_____
5. Turning cards—Average (per blot)	1 turn	2 turns	3 turns	4 turns	_____
6. Action responses—Average (per blot)	1	2	3	5	_____
7. Creative responses	0	1	2	4	_____
8. Conventional responses	25	30	35	45	_____
9. Human responses	6	13	22	30	_____
10. Animal responses	18	24	24	24	_____
11. Object responses	4	3	2	2	_____
12. Sexual responses	0	1	2	4	_____
13. Fearful responses	1	2	3	5	_____
14. Nature responses	3	4	6	9	_____

Conclusions: The preceding chart allows you to compare your results with those of others who have taken these tests. When you complete the column, "Reader's Responses," you can determine how you rank, from low average to very high above average. Fifteen categories are provided, each with a variety of descriptions about one's personality. These categories provide information as follows:

1. **Total Responses**—the larger the number, the greater the imagination, therefore the greater the potential for creativity. Imaginative people frequently want to change some aspect of the world around them.

2. **Total Blot Responses**—larger responses, where the total blot is used, suggest good organizing ability and a potential for abstract thinking.

3 & 4. **Small-area Responses**—show flexibility. As the ratio of large (or total-blot responses) goes up, so does the ability to compromise.

5. **Turning Blots**—the more turns, the greater the energy level.

6. **Action responses**—these are responses wherein the animals or humans are seen in action. This denotes an active person. However, it is important also to note whether the action is combative or friendly. This shows the type of action the person dreams about, but not necessarily engages in.

7. **Creative Responses**—these are responses not seen by the majority of other people. This type of response indicates an ability to show originality.

8. **Conventional Responses**—are those seen by others according to the listings. A high percentage of matching responses correlates with conventional fantasy.

9. **Human Responses**—show an interest in the thinking and action of other people.

10. **Animal Responses**—show an ability to engage in casual fantasy.

11. **Object Responses**—show practical thinking, often related to work interest.

12. **Sexual Responses**—reflect an ability to discuss sexual ideas and a general interest in sexual activity.

13. **Fearful Responses**—indicate a desire to talk about things that are fearful.

14. **Nature Responses**—reflect an interest in the outdoors and the world of nature.

15. **Weapon Responses**—may reflect an interest in combat.

From this listing, you can find much information about your personality. This test was not, however, designed to determine personality weakness. It is *not* of the same type as the famous inkblot test used by psychologists in a clinical setting. That test requires considerable interpretive skills and utilizes a much different and more complicated scoring technique.

Handwriting Analysis

No book on testing would be complete without a section on handwriting analysis. Handwriting is one of the few testable human activities that takes place every day. Thus, with some knowledge of handwriting analysis, a person can get an almost daily check of mood changes and personality variations. Have you ever wondered whether you were in a mood to be able to make important decisions? Have you sometimes felt that you were depressed, and yet you weren't sure? Do you know when you feel most secure? This section should help answer these and other important questions concerning personality functioning.

Not too long ago, I knew virtually nothing about handwriting analysis and would have had to classify myself as a skeptic of that analytic method. Then, in early 1977, I became involved in testing applicants for police and security jobs. In the course of this work, I met Rose Matousek and for the first time saw handwriting analysis in operation. The company I work with, Personnel Security Corporation, has a highly sophisticated testing program and I, therefore, had a valid yardstick against which to measure Rose's analyses. To say the least, her evaluations were phenomenal.

My interest was aroused, and I began checking Rose's work against my own clinical testing results. As the data began to pour in, it became clear that handwriting analysis can be extremely accurate; at least, it appeared that Rose's work was. At times, it almost seemed magical!

However, as I studied more thoroughly, I came to find that handwriting analysis is scientific; it has a body of data supporting it and has carefully spelled out rules of procedure. Thus, a section on this fascinating science, prepared by Rose Matousek (who also has written a manual on handwriting analysis, called **Graphodynamics**), is included in this book.

Handwriting Analysis Tests

Handwriting analysis is widely accepted in Europe where one of the first treatises on the subject was written by an Italian physician, Camillo Baldi, in 1632. European psychologists, psychiatrists, criminologists, physicians, attorneys and personnel administrators have since established it as a valuable tool in determining personality characteristics. In fact, many European universities require a course in graphology as part of the curriculum for a Ph.D. in psychology.

Graphology does not have that kind of foothold in the United States.

Some physicians have used it in the diagnosis of Parkinson's disease, cancer, and other ailments which affect brain cells; a scattered few have attempted to advance it, such as Dr. Werner Wolff, a professor at Bard College who wrote **Diagrams of the Unconscious**, and Dr. Ulrich Sonneman, a clinical psychologist who wrote **Handwriting Analysis as a Psychodiagnostic Tool.** If American business uses it for personnel purposes, rarely is it publicized.

Handwriting has been dubbed "brain writing" because brain impulses are recorded in our writing much as heart impulses are in electrocardiogram charts. If for some reason you were to lose the use of your dominant hand, the same characteristics would appear in any writing you might do with a pen in your opposite hand, your mouth, your toes, or whatever way you chose to write.

Dr. Wolff, in **Diagrams of the Unconscious,** gives evidence after 30 years of signature research that there are elements of writing which remain consistent throughout a person's lifetime. Other studies have shown that writing gestures correspond to your other gestures and to your attitudes. The environment, culture, and teachings to which you're exposed have an impact on your writing, but it's your particular inner workings which make your writing different from anyone else's and as distinctive as a fingerprint.

Take the following tests; you'll find them revealing.

—Rose Matousek

A. How Do You Feel About Yourself?

Score

1. What size are your small letters—those without upper or lower loops?

a. Small
1-3 mm.
This is small writing.   1

b. Average
3mm.
This is average.   2

c. Tall
3½ mm. or more
This is tall   3

d. Variable
All sizes
This is variable   0

2. How tall are your capitals?

a. Short
1 to 2 times
your small letters
Chicago, Illinois   1

b. Average
2 to 3 times
your small letters
Chicago, Illinois   2

c. Tall 3 times or more
the size of your
small letters
Chicago, Illinois   3

d. Variable
All sizes
Chicago, Illinois   0

3. How tall is your personal pronoun "I"?

a. Short
Shorter than your
other capitals
I'll call in April.   1

b. Average
As tall as your
other capitals
I'll call in April.   2

c. Tall
Taller than your
other capitals
I'll call in April.   3

d. Variable
All sizes
I'll call in April   0

Total Score _____

Evaluation

A. How Do You Feel About Yourself?

Score	Determination
8-9	Abundant ego
5-7	Good substantial ego
3-4	Ego needs a boost
0-2	Get help!

Your real self-estimate is revealed in your lower-case letters because they show whether you operate with confidence or with insecurity. If they're of average size, you have a secure self-regard, but if they're smaller, you're not quite so confident. You have no qualms about yourself if they're taller than average. But, if they bounce around in size, your ego is going through the same exercise. Some days you feel great; on others your spirits sag mightily.

Capitals reveal your superficial ego. As you start your sentences, you put a great deal of conscious effort into it and put your best foot forward, so to speak, in its beginning with the capital. When your capitals are very tall, your're trying to impress the beholder to make that person think you're rising to the heights. If they are small, you're being modest. When they're average, you're not trying to fool anyone but are just being honest.

Your personal pronoun "I" holds your personal self-worth. It's a most unusual word in that it's the only personal pronoun in the world written with one letter and also capitalized. No other written personal pronoun has that unique distinction. If it's very tall, and especially if it's wider and more flourished, you're strutting like a peacock spreading its full tail. If it's small and simple in design, you're modest but probably insecure.

B. Are You Displaying A Facade?

Score

1. Does your signature measure up to your regular writing?

a. Smaller signature than your regular writing   1

b. Same size signature as your regular writing   2

c. Larger signature than your regular writing   3

2. How do you distinguish your signature?

a. You don't; it's the same as your regular writing   1

b. With underlinings and/or with flourishes   2

c. With an illegible scrawl   3

3. What size are the initials of your signature?

a. Same size as the capitals in your regular writing   1

b. Given name capital larger than surname capital   2

c. Surname capital larger than given name capital   3

Total Score _____

Evaluation

B. Are You Displaying A Facade?
 Score   Determination
 3-4   You're a natural
 5-6   Putting someone on
 7-9   Putting on the dog

Your signature expresses your feeling of importance, but it especially indicates the impression you'd like others to have of you. In a small signature, there's no display of importance, but in a large signature the visual impact is far greater.

If your signature is larger than the way you normally write, you may be overcompensating for inferiority feelings; if it's smaller, you'd like to suppress how you feel about yourself so that you don't overpower others.

A flourished signature indicates a show-off, and an illegible signature screams out that you don't want anybody to know who you really are and what you're really all about.

The initials in your signature are tell-tales of how you feel in relation to your family background. Your given name represents you, and yours is a strong ego if the initial of your given name is extra large. If the capital of your surname is extraordinarily large, you attach a great deal of importance to family, heritage, and the like.

For example, if you're a married woman and your given-name initial is much taller than your husband's surname, it would be highly likely that you are: 1. not happy in your marriage, or 2. superior in your own mind to your husband's family.

C. Are You Governed By Your Emotions?

                                                                                              Score

1. What do you use primarily in your writing?

    a. Printing   *Hello everyone*   1

    b. Straight lines and angles   *Hello everyone*   2

    c. Curves with straight
       lines and angles   *Hello everyone*   3

    d. All curves and loops   *Hello everyone*   4

2. What's the slant of your writing?

    a. Vertical   *This is vertical.*   1

    b. Left   *This is left slanted.*   2

    c. Right   *This is right slanted.* 3

    d. Variable   *This is variable.*   4

3. What's your writing pressure?

    a. Light   *This is light.*   1

    b. Medium   *This is medium.*   2

    c. Heavy   *This is heavy.*   3

    d. Extra heavy with embossing
       on the reverse side of the paper *This is extra heavy.*   4

4. How do the lines of your writing run?

    a. Straight   *This is straight*   1

    b. Rising   *This is rising.*   2

    c. Falling   *This is falling.*   3

    d. Wavy or rolling   *This is wavy and rolling* 4

                                                      Total Score ____

Evaluation

C. Are You Governed By Your Emotions?

Score	Determination
4- 6	Super control
7-10	Good control
11-13	So-so control
14-16	Emotionally wrought up

A preference for straight lines and angles shows a disciplined nature. It takes a great deal of control to come to an abrupt stop and make an about face in the direction of writing when making an angle. Curves are softer and easier.

If you have a consistent slant, this indicates good control. However, if you're slanting to the left sometimes and to the right at other times, you're out of control. Right slanted writing is what generally is taught in school because it is the most comfortable for most. It requires concentration to write vertically or backhand.

Those who have extreme pressure bury their pen or pencil in the paper for a lasting impression. That's how their emotions are—lasting. Those who write with less pressure slough off their emotions more readily than heavy pressured writers, although their emotions can run as strong but not necessarily as long.

If your lines move straight across the page, you're in control. If they rise, you're buoyant and optimistic. If the lines fall, you're either fatigued or depressed. If they continue to go downhill after a good night's rest, see a shrink fast. Look out if they're wavy lines because that means you're very moody and unpredictable.

D. What's Your Drive?

1. Which design pleases you?

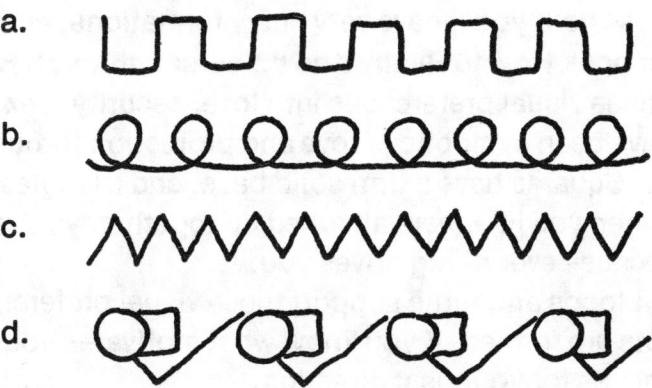

2. How do you dot your "i's"?

a. precisely over the stem

b. with circles

c. with diacritics

d. high flying and dashed

3. How do you take your turns when making loops?

a. according to copybook

b. with added roundness

c. with angles

d. with extra long and full sweeps

Score:
No. of a's____
No. of b's____
No. of c's____
No. of d's____

Evaluation

D. **What's Your Drive?**

Score	Determination
2-3 a's	Motivated by security
2-3 b's	Motivated by love
2-3 c's	Motivated by sex
2-3 d's	Motivated by your imagination

It's interesting to note that what pleases you visually usually will be incorporated into your writing. If you enjoy the teepee formations, you'll use a lot of angles. If circles please you, you'll have very curvy formations, and so on.

Shirl Solomon, in her book **How to Really Know Yourself through Handwriting,** breaks down these visual preferences into love, security, sex and imagination. Circles have been symbolic of love and protection throughout cultures, art and poetry. Squares have a firm solid base, and triangles very often symbolize sex. When you like them all rolled up together, you've got the best thing going because everything drives you.

The formation of your loops and turns support these visual preferences, as do the way your i-dots are formed. If you know what motivates you, you'll be able to set your compass for your best direction.

5. Tests of Sexual Interests, Knowledge and Preferences

1. A Test of Sexual Knowledge
2. A Pictorial Ranking of Women
3. A Pictorial Ranking of Men
4. A Woman's Test of Sexual Attraction
5. A Man's Test of Sexual Attraction

These tests were designed primarily for fun, but they should also prove informative. Increased knowledge in an important area of human functioning should make life a little more enjoyable. We also believe that taking these tests with a loved one may well improve communication. As that happens, the relationship should deepen. At least, we hope so.

A Test of Sexual Knowledge

Our contemporary times often have been called "the age of sexual enlightenment," probably because there exists so much dialogue about sexuality. The big concern today seems to be whether one is sufficiently active to be considered normal! People also are concerned with the abundance of their knowledge.

Yet, with all of the so-called "openness," there still exists much misinformation. Often, there seems more talk than pleasure and enlightenment.

Is there, for example, a real understanding of how to establish successful foreplay, of how nudity, temperature and fantasy affect sexual performance, of the critical factors that underlie extramarital affairs? Even the causes of impotence and frigidity often are poorly understood. This test allows the reader to evaluate his or her knowledge. In that sense it should provide enlightenment.

Instructions: Select what you feel is the best answer to each of the following questions (or in some cases, provide an answer). Then check your answers against those provided at the conclusion of the test.

1. What is the number of sperm in one ejaculation from the average male?

a. 500 to 800
b. 750,000 to 1,000,000
c. 300,000 to 700,000
d. 400,000,000 to 500,000,000

2. Is there a correlation between amount of sexual activity and education?

    Yes   No

3. The greatest percent increase in venereal disease is among those in which age group?

a. 11-15
b. 16-19
c. 20-22
d. adults

4. Does temperature affect love making?

    Yes   No

5. How long do sperm live inside a woman's body?

a. 12-15 hours
b. 24-48 hours
c. 3-4 days
d. 1 week

6. Men are turned on by nude pictures to a far greater degree than are women turned on by such pictures.

    True   False

7. With what group of men is premature ejaculation most likely to occur?

8. Is there a non-medical treatment for premature ejaculation?

9. There has been a substantial increase in homosexuality of late.

    True   False

10. When a man and a woman are attracted to each other, generally they wear similar clothing.

   True   False

11. Studies show that the American executive becomes involved in extra-marital affairs at a higher rate than the general population.

   True   False

12. Do women ejaculate during orgasm?

13. Women are marrying at a younger age than ever before.

   True   False

14. Are there changes in the female breast during excitement?

   Yes   No

15. Americans are the most sexually preoccupied people in the world.

   Yes   No

16. There is a wide discrepancy between what children believe to be the frequency of their parents' sexual activity and what it actually is or has been.

   Yes   No

17. There is danger that if a woman becomes tense her vagina may hold the penis so that separation is extremely difficult.

   True   False

18. Blowing into the genital organs can be very dangerous.

   Yes   No

19. What is a dildo?

20. What are skin gloves and skin thimbles?

21. Mutual or simultaneous orgasm should be the ultimate goal of love making.

   True   False

22. On the average, how long does it take each sex to reach an orgasm?

23. Most of the couples who exchange partners with others claim poor marriages.

   True   False

24. Wild sexual fantasies during love making are damaging because they detract from the reality of the situation.

   True   False

25. Approximately what percentage of women regularly reach orgasm during intercourse?

a. 30%
b. 40%
c. 50%
d. 60%

26. What is the approximate percentage of male sexual problems that are caused by organic difficulties?

a. 60%
b. 40%
c. 20%
d. 10%

27. What are the most common errors of technique made by women in their foreplay?

28. Is penis size important to success in love making?

   Yes   No   Perhaps

29. To bring the woman to climax, the man must adjust his position so that his penis comes in contact with the clitoris.

   Yes   No

30. Oral sex is dangerous and unhealthy.

   True   False

31. Does sexual activity stop in later life?

32. Masturbation is a destructive act because it causes withdrawal from contact with others.

   True   False

33. Is there discomfort when an orgasm has not been reached?

34. What is the major cause of impotence and frigidity?

35. Why is penis size difficult to determine?

36. Are men able to be multi-orgasmic?

   Yes   No

37. Can women actually reach more than one orgasm during intercourse?

   Yes   No

38. What is the best way to insure a good sex life?

39. Is alcohol helpful to sexual performance?

   Yes   No

40. Is a woman's sexual drive as strong as a man's?

   Yes   No

Scoring: After you have recorded your answers, compare them with those that are provided. Each fully correct answer counts two points, for a total possible score of 80 points. Each person must make his or her own judgments as to whether he or she has obtained a correct score (two points), a partially correct score (one point) or whether he or she has failed that question (zero points). After scoring is completed, check the analysis of your performance which follows after answer number forty.

Answers to Questions:
1. d. 400,000,000-500,000,000—not as high as some males would like to believe, but certainly adequate!

2. Yes—especially for women. Educated women are more apt to become sexually involved before marriage and to try a greater variety of sexual acts.

With men, the difference is not as great, but better educated men are more active.

3. a. Alarming as this sounds, the very young now are most vulnerable to venereal disease. Their rate of increase in disease is the highest.

4. Yes, it certainly seems to be a fact, because many studies show that frequency of intercourse decreases as the temperature drops below 70° F.

5. b. Generally for 24 to 48 hours, but in rare cases slightly longer.

6. False—men are more responsive to nude pictures than are women but, according to recent studies, women have closed the gap. The differences now are not great.

7. Generally, young men in their late teens and early twenties.

8. Yes, by applying pressure with the fingers just below the glans.

9. False. Recent studies show about the same figure (8%) as was found in earlier studies. There just exists more talk about it!

10. True—surprising as it may sound, the tendency is for both sexes to wear clothing that is more open at the neck.

11. False—although we have come to expect such to be the case due to sensational articles, recent studies show that only 20% of executives stray.

12. No—in all probability the idea that women ejaculate evolves from fantasy—at least, so say the majority of experts.

13. False—the median age for females to marry now is 21 as compared with age 20 in the 1950s and 1960s.

14. Yes—the nipples become erect and the breasts enlarge somewhat due to increased blood supply.

15. No, surprising as that may sound. We are loaded with sexually oriented advertisements, but studies show that many other nationalities actually spend more time thinking of sex.

16. Absolutely yes. Daughters are more inaccurate (on the low side) than sons, but children of both sexes believe their parents to be much less active than they are or have been.

17. False—a myth that has helped produce unnecessary anxiety.

18. Yes. It can cause embolism with the female and damage to the small canals in the male.

19. Dildos are artificial penises.

20. They are gloves of various textures or finger cots similar in size to a sewing thimble that are used for erotic massage.

21. False—the ultimate goal should be mutual pleasure, which each partner generally achieves as long as each reaches orgasm at some time during the act of love.

22. Men about three minutes, women about 12 minutes.

23. False—at least, so they say. These "swingers," as they are called, claim to be happily married.

24. False—nearly all experts agree that fantasy is very common and probably enriches the experience.

25. a. 30%

26. d. 10%, diabetes being one of the more common causes.

27. Not pressing with sufficient force and not pressing at the base of the penis.

28. A very difficult question to answer. From a purely anatomical point of view, "no," because the vagina is flexible and adapts to varying sized penises. However, if one has a negative psychological feeling about the size of the penis, then the answer is "yes." Probably, "no" is the best answer because that is the one given by the majority of women.

29. No—the vagina adjusts and as a result there is automatic clitoral contact.

30. False—it is healthy if both partners enjoy it. One other interesting fact—the bacteria content is higher in the mouth than in the genitals.

31. Many people report an active sex life in their seventies, eighties, and even nineties. Good health and favorable partners are important. Fun breeds more fun!

32. False—some therapists have even encouraged masturbation as a means of starting one toward reaching an initial orgasm.

33. Yes, because the blood that has flowed into the sexual organs has not been partially expelled as happens with orgasm. Vasocongestion (the physiological term) is rapidly relieved with orgasm.

34. Anxiety, fear and/or guilt reactions. Basically, though, anxiety causes these problems.

35. Generally, because penis size usually is determined by the size in the flaccid state where there is great variability. The small penis enlarges much more with erection than does the large penis (judged in the flaccid state) and with erection generally there are not great differences in penis size.

36. Only a small percent (less than 15%) and generally only with the very young males.

37. Many women are able to reach a number of orgasms in one session.

38. Make it comfortable, mutually fun and one part of a good relationship.

39. Alcohol may temporarily reduce fear, but in the long run it diminishes sexual prowess.

40. Nearly all current research indicates that when anxiety is reduced and women are given encouragement to respond, their sexual drive equals that of men.

Analysis

Total Points	Rating
75-80	An Expert
70-74	Excellent Knowledge
65-69	Very Good
60-64	Average
55-59	Below Average
50-54	Well Below Average
49 and below	Very Poor Performance

Conclusion: Now that you have completed the test, you have an idea how your knowledge stacks up. That should help clarify what your weak areas are and where your knowledge is strong. Self knowledge can aid toward self growth. If your knowledge is high, you can feel more confident; if it is limited, you may want to read some of the fine books now available on the market. Or you may decide that, after all, you have sufficient knowledge to accomplish what you want.

A Pictorial Ranking of Women: FOR MEN ONLY

Introduction: It is a well known fact that people often repeatedly select the same type of partner, even though that selection causes dissatisfaction. This happens because selections often are dictated by the unconscious mind.

When a man selects a woman he reflects a good deal of his personality. Quite frequently that man is pulled toward a type of woman very different from what he feels he wants. For example, I have seen men who talked long and loud about how the women they want must be assertive, warm and outgoing. Yet they seem to select women who are quiet, inhibited and passive. Is it possible that unconsciously they want women they are able to dominate? Does their insecurity dictate their choice? Can these men possibly be happy with women far from their conscious ideal?

This test is designed to shed some light upon the processes involved when a man selects a lady. A man taking the test should gain knowledge about himself and about what unconsciously he seems to find appealing.

138

Instructions: There are nine pictures of women in a variety of poses. Look carefully at each of the drawings and then select your first, second and third favorites. An analysis of the results is presented immediately following the pictures.

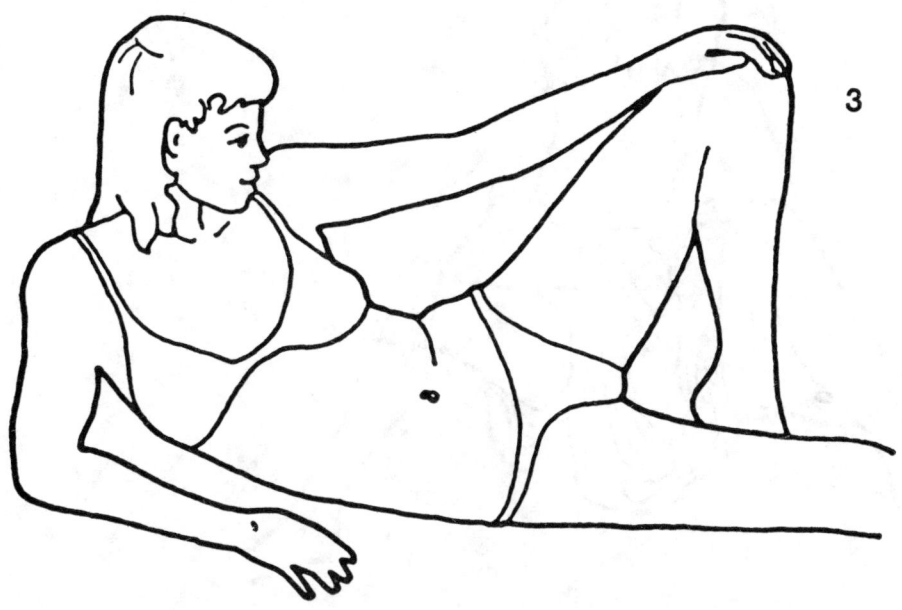

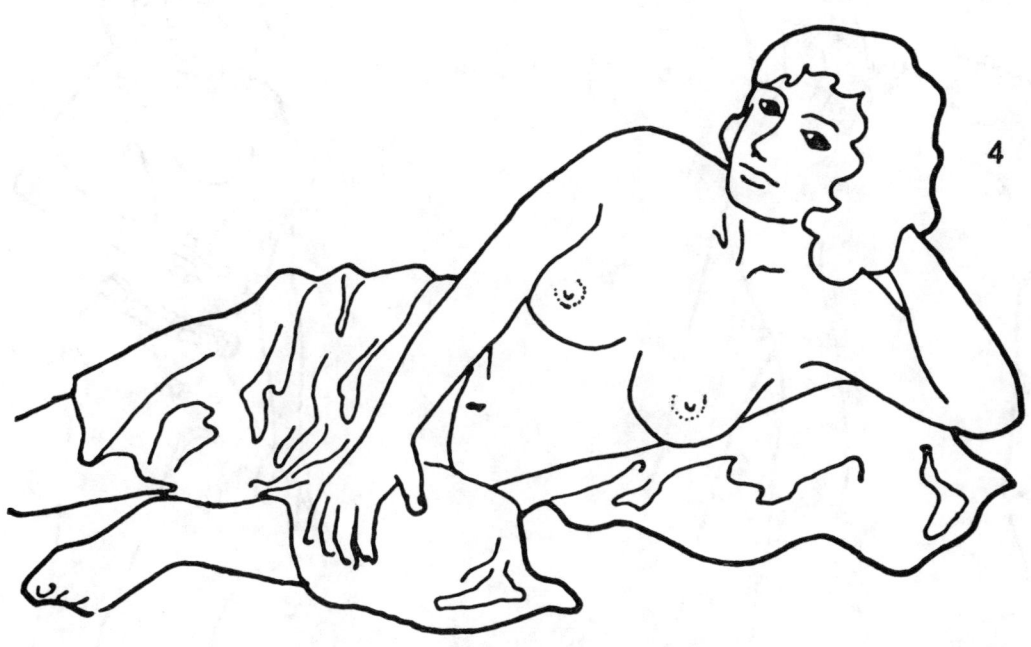

140

5

6

7

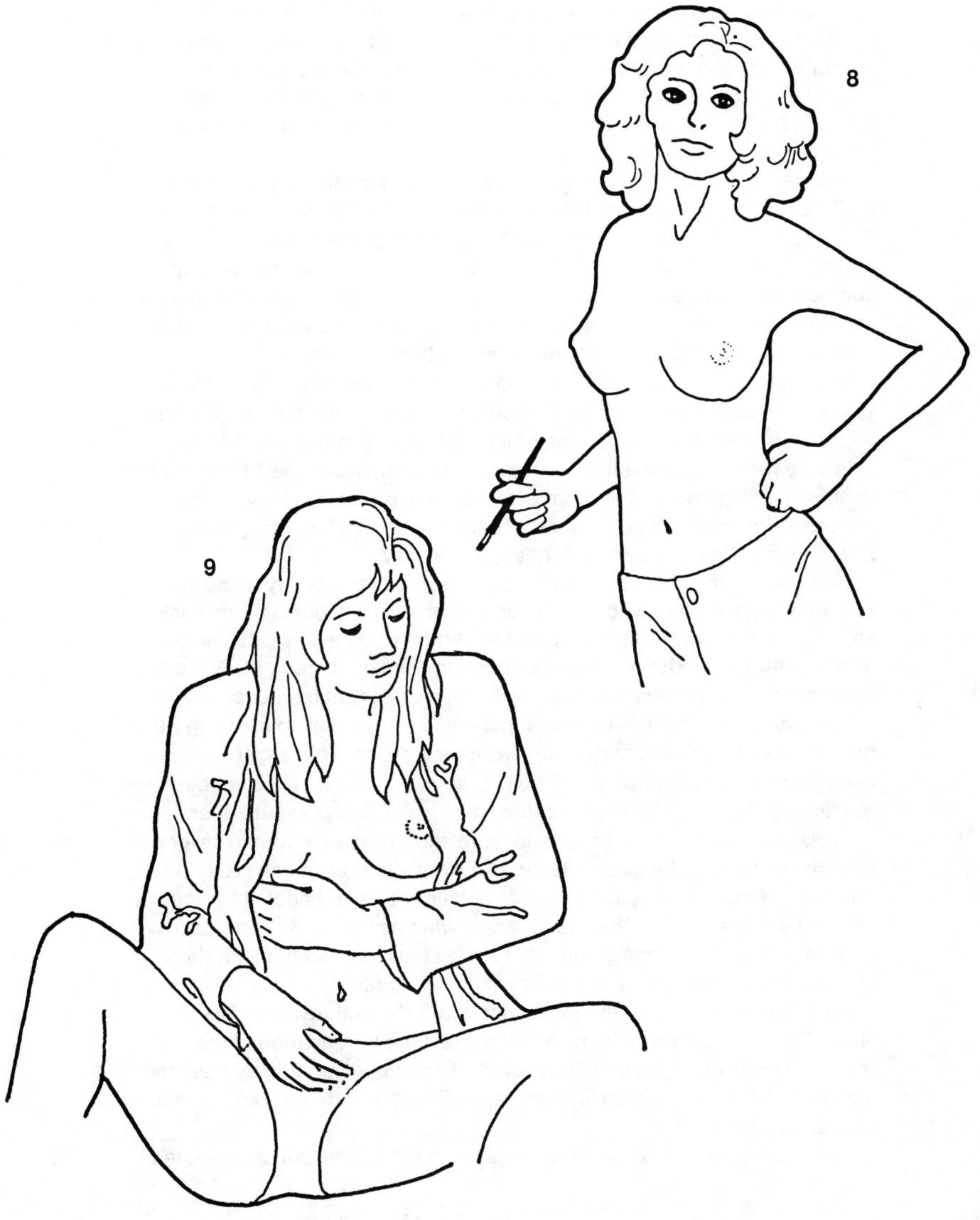

Scoring: You were asked to select three of the nine pictures presented in this test and to rank them in order of preference. These same pictures were evaluated by a group of psychiatrists, psychologists and artists and ultimately placed in groups of three. There was rather close agreement between the professionals as to the characteristics represented in each picture.

The women in pictures 1, 2 and 3 were judged to be shy and somewhat inhibited. this group arbitrarily was assigned as the "left grouping." Pictures 4, 5 and 6 were judged to portray outgoing, available and mildly assertive women. This became the "middle grouping." The "right group" is composed of pictures 7, 8 and 9. These pictures represent women judged to be highly aggressive, challenging to men and inclined to want things their way. They may be basically shy but they use bravado to cover up.

Your three selections tell something about your sexual preferences. Do you wish to have a secure, highly responsive woman (middle group), or do you wish to dominate (left group), or be dominated (right group)? Those selecting the middle will allow women to respond. They expect their women to enjoy making love, but to be selective and have a direct voice in what happens. They want a 50-50 partner. These will be playful, non-game-playing men. They will be direct, open, and warm.

Choices at either end of the continuum suggest uncertainty in the male. It becomes a question of who dominates. Since the shy woman holds back, she won't put a shy male to the test. Those men who are shy will feel more - secure. The same exists with the dominating woman at the right. Since she directs the action, she is responsible for everything that happens.

There are three possible rankings that could be made by men taking this test: 1. They may select one picture from each group. This suggests an inability to make up one's mind. The first selection shows a desire, but it is not likely to be easily fulfilled because there is a pull in opposite directions. Uncertainty characterizes this relationship and this man's woman never will know how to act. 2. All three selections may be pictures in one grouping. This type of man knows what he wants and he will be unhappy if he doesn't get it. His women also rather clearly know what he wants. 3. Two pictures may be selected from one group. This shows less consistency, but there still is a rather strong push toward one kind of woman.

Nonetheless, the most revealing selection is the picture ranked as No. 1. That will tell the main push. Then it is merely a question of the pulls in the opposite direction and the amount of conflict generated by a second and third choice. Inconsistency breeds conflict, for both the man and the woman involved.

Too much conflict may cause both partners to become unhappy. Instead of trying to force a lady friend into a role, a man might do better to consider altering his own personality. A personality change should result in changing the man's selection process. It also should help him become more consistent in what he wants from his woman. Asking dominance one moment and submissiveness the next only confuses a woman. This places immense strain upon the relationship.

A Pictorial Ranking of Men: FOR WOMEN ONLY

Introduction: Many women find themselves attracted to the same kind of men over and over again. Quite frequently these women find themselves in a relationship that feels just like one they recently ended. They wonder how it happened to them again.

There also are large numbers of women who have no clear idea of what sort of men attract them. Sure, they recognize some of the surface qualities, but they are not aware of the inner qualities of the men that attract them.

Women often ask themselves questions such as, "Why did I find that man attractive?" Or, "I wonder why I felt such a strong pull toward that guy?" On more rare occasions, a truly frank woman may state that she is not altogether sure what she is seeking.

There has been much psychological data to suggest that a lady's personality determines what she finds attractive in a man. Is she looking for a man to dominate her because she feels so helpless herself? Or does she seek a timid man because she is afraid to lose control? Sometimes a woman is pulled in several different directions at the same time. She needs warmth, but is afraid that if she finds a warm, erotic man she will lose him to a more adequate woman. Which need will predominate? Her need to feel secure and hold onto a shy man? Or her need to share warmth with a man? Does the shy woman need an outgoing man to complement her shyness? Or does she need a man who will share her shyness?

Perhaps, as a lady better understands herself and her needs, she will find that her relationships become more rational. It then may become possible to ask more consistently for what she truly wants.

Instructions: This test is composed of nine drawings of men in different poses. Take a good look at each drawing and then select your first, second and third favorites. An analysis of the results is presented immediately following the pictures.

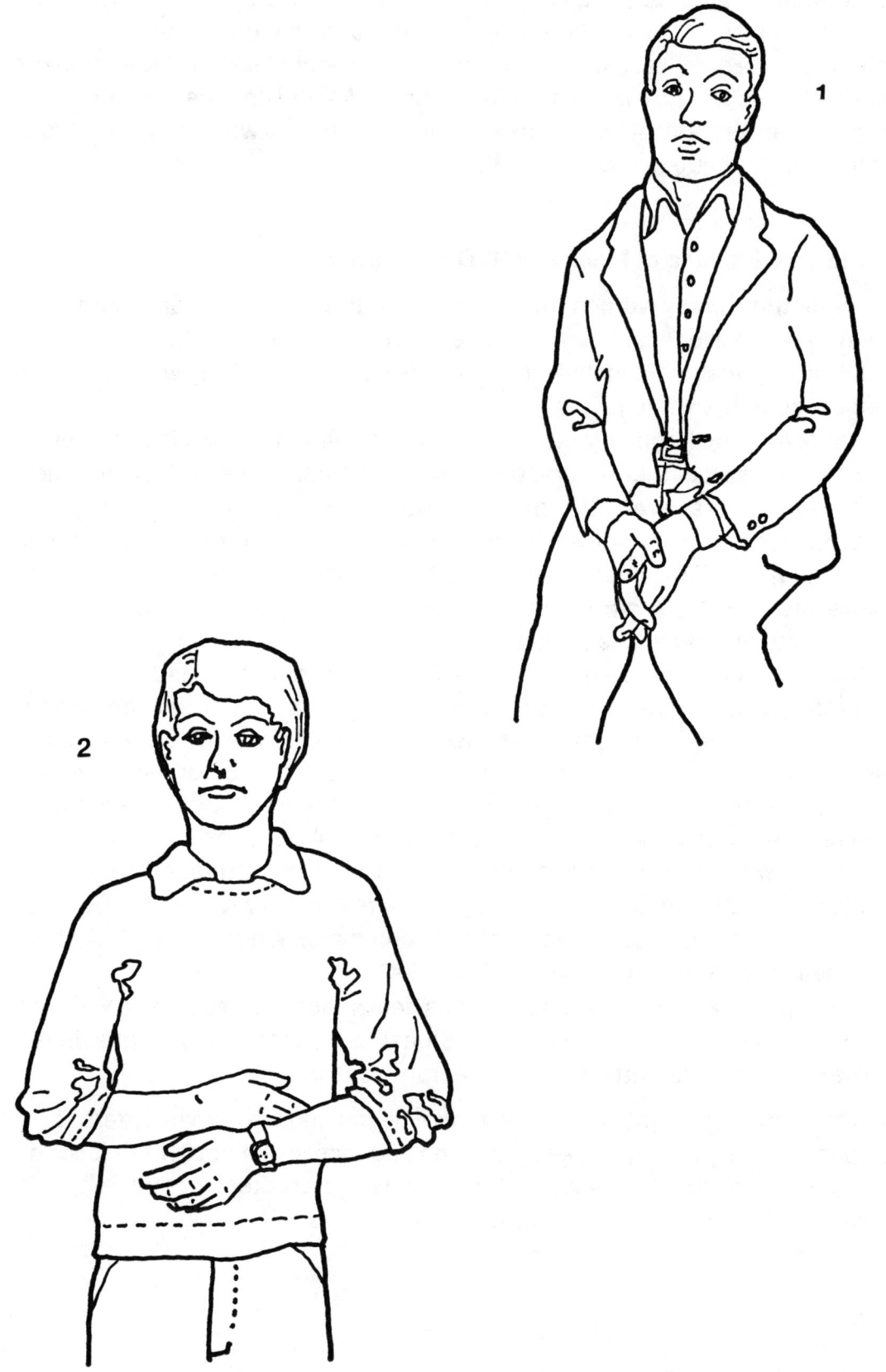

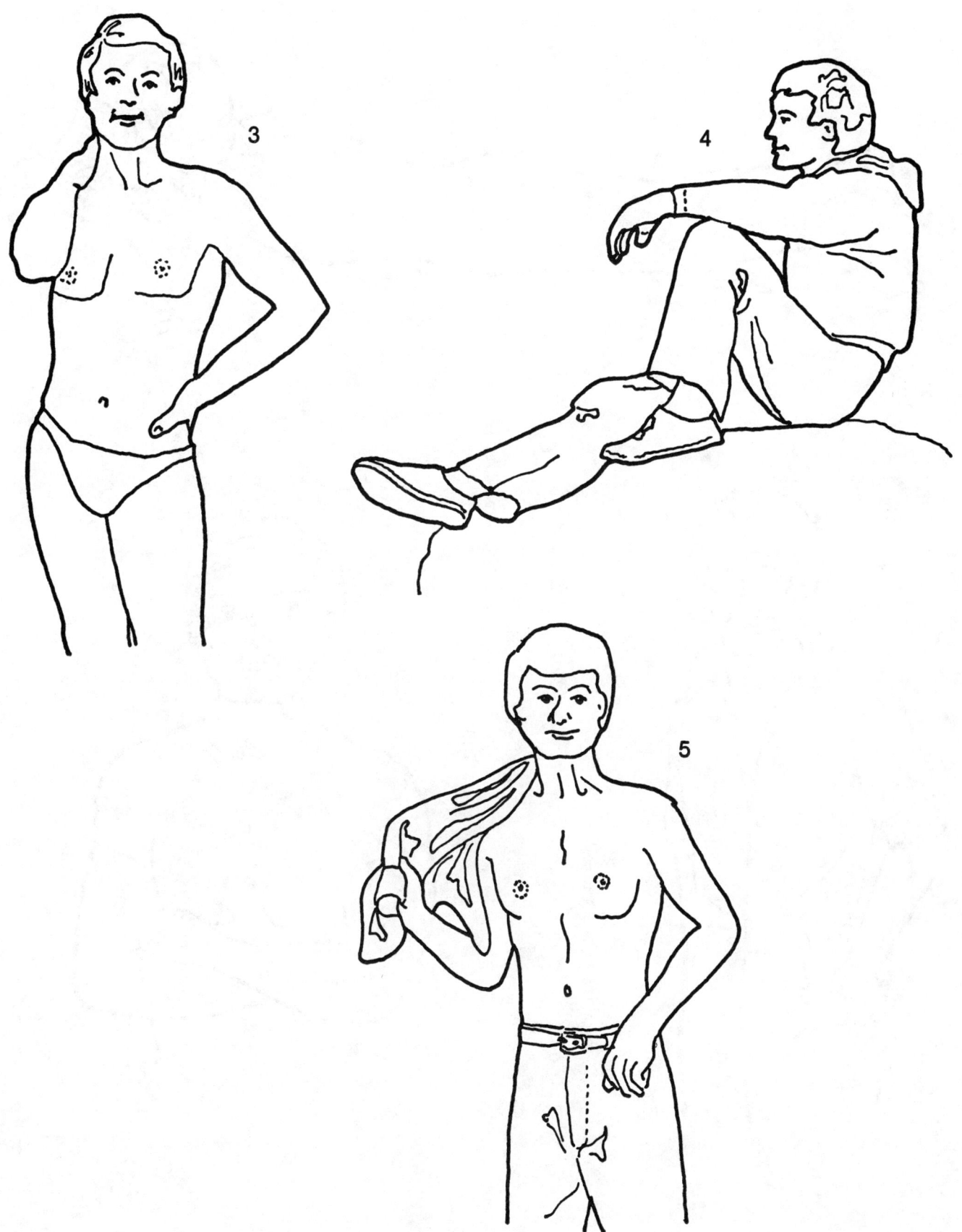

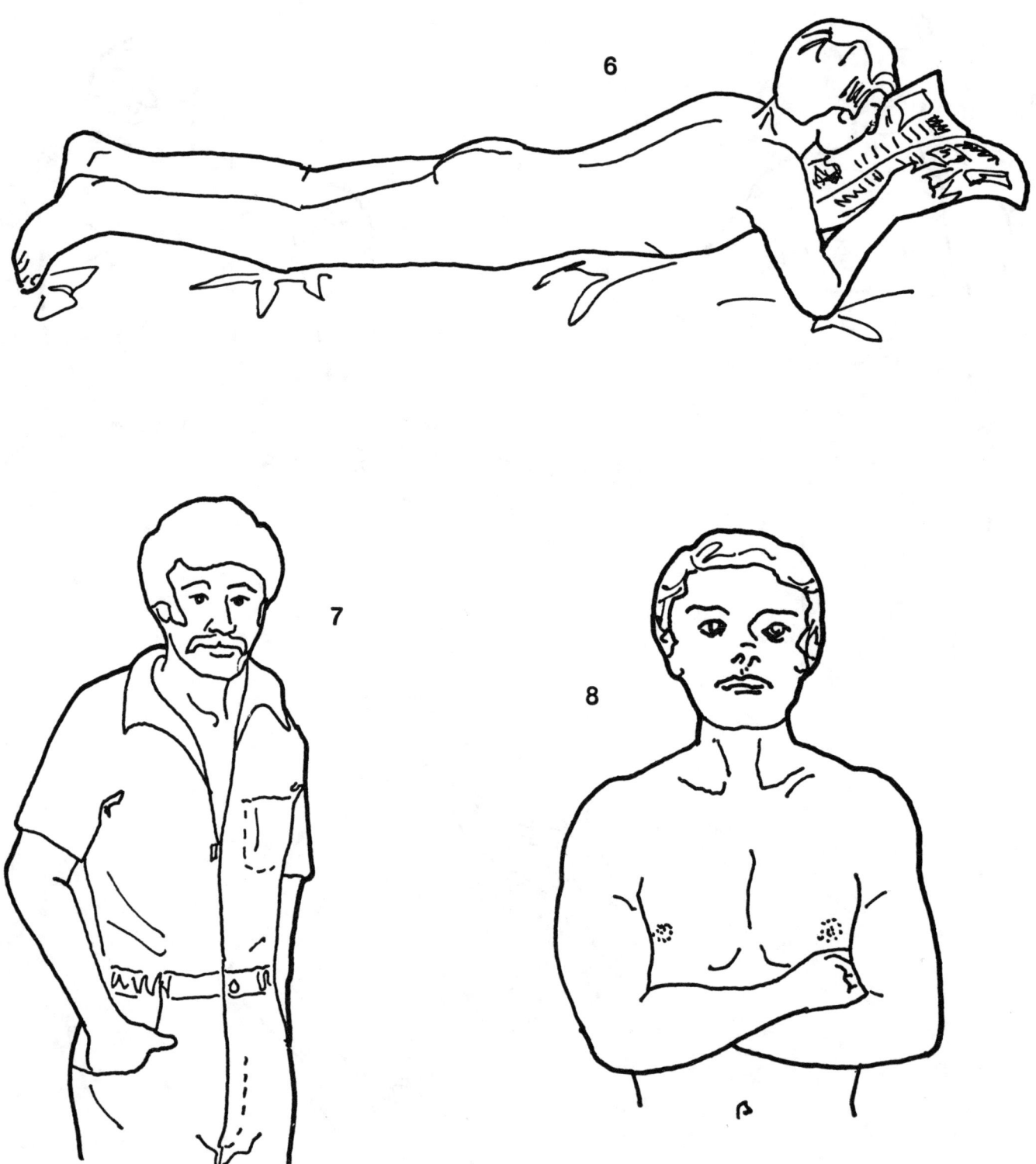

9

Scoring: This test was constructed in the same manner as the one designed for men. The nine pictures were ranked by teams of psychologists, psychiatrists and artists as depicting certain personality traits. Finally, three groups were established, arbitrarily called the "left," "right" and "middle" groups.

The "left" group is composed of pictures 1, 2 and 3, and depicts men who are shy, passive and generally inhibited. These men would expect their women to either (a.) also be shy or (b.) dominate them. The middle group, consisting of pictures 4, 5 and 6, represents assertive, warm, confident and outgoing men. They are direct and, as such, are not game-players. They can be playful, but they expect their women to share equally in their pleasures. The right group, represented by pictures 7, 8 and 9, are dominating, highly aggressive men. They may be insecure but they hide their uncertainty with bravado.

Meaning of Selections: The first choice is, of course, the most important. It tells what the basic desire is and how the woman prefers to be treated. Of equal importance, though, is the representation of each group. Three choices that fall within the same group indicate a very dominant, consistent desire to interact in one way. There is less conflict with such a choice. Selecting one man from each of the three categories indicates uncertainty and, therefore, changing behavior. The lady simply can't make up her mind what she wants. One minute she wants to share, the next minute she wishes to dominate, and, later, to be dominated. Confusion will reign, but her first choice is the strongest, i.e., that which she most ideally desires.

Two selections within one category tell the prevalent desire, but if the No. 1 selection isn't one of the two matching choices, the woman will be confused and confusing. She then is revealing the many sides of her personality. However, in ranking her preferences, she can, at least, see in what direction she is most strongly pulled. Making these desires more conscious should provide a clearer picture of what she is seeking. In so doing, perhaps the conflict can be reduced.

No one should expect a test to make magic changes; a personality does not suddenly become altered. However, you may now be better able to understand your conflicts. Perhaps these different needs could even be shared with one man if he is someone special and understanding. He just may be able to play slightly different roles at different times.

A Woman's Test of Sexual Attraction
FOR WOMEN ONLY

Introduction: Do you know which of a man's physical characteristics first attract you? Are you aware that each woman is different in regards to what turns her on? Did you know that many women who claim they prefer men with hair on their chests actually select men without body hair?

A lady's personality does have an influence upon what she finds attractive. For example, women who desire aggressive men often believe that they should select men of rugged appearance. With this false belief, they often are disappointed with their selections.

This test measures what it is that you really prefer. It helps take the guesswork out of stating what you like. For that reason, it should prove interesting. It not only should be fun but also should tell you something about what you like in men, and what you are like yourself.

Instructions: This test shows areas of the male body and the purpose is to determine which parts are given greater emphasis by women. The instructions are simple: Ladies are asked to pick the two pictures of the seven that they prefer, stating their first and second choices. Some may wish to rank all seven in order of preference and that is fine, too. After you make your selections, turn to the scoring section to see how you rate.

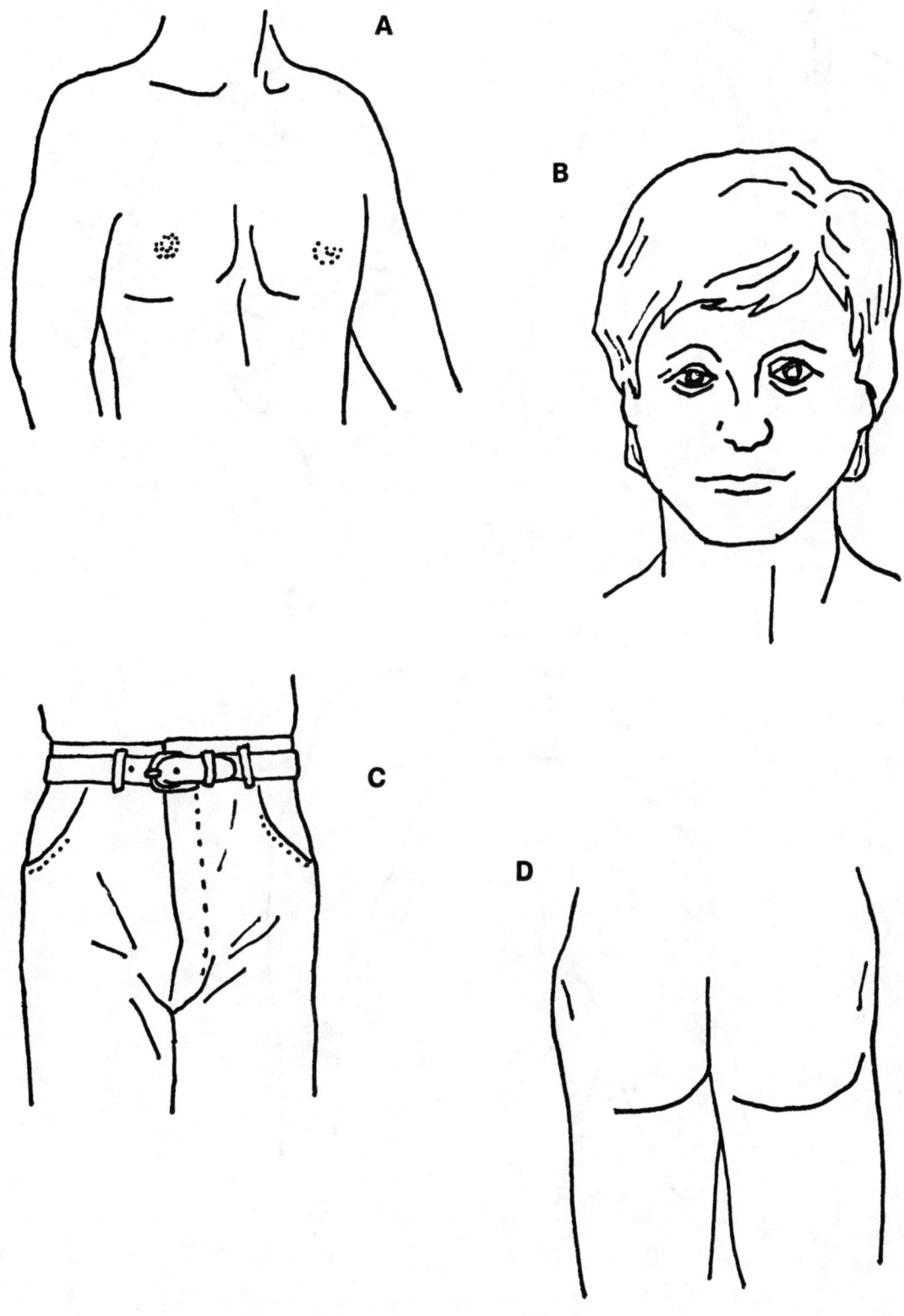

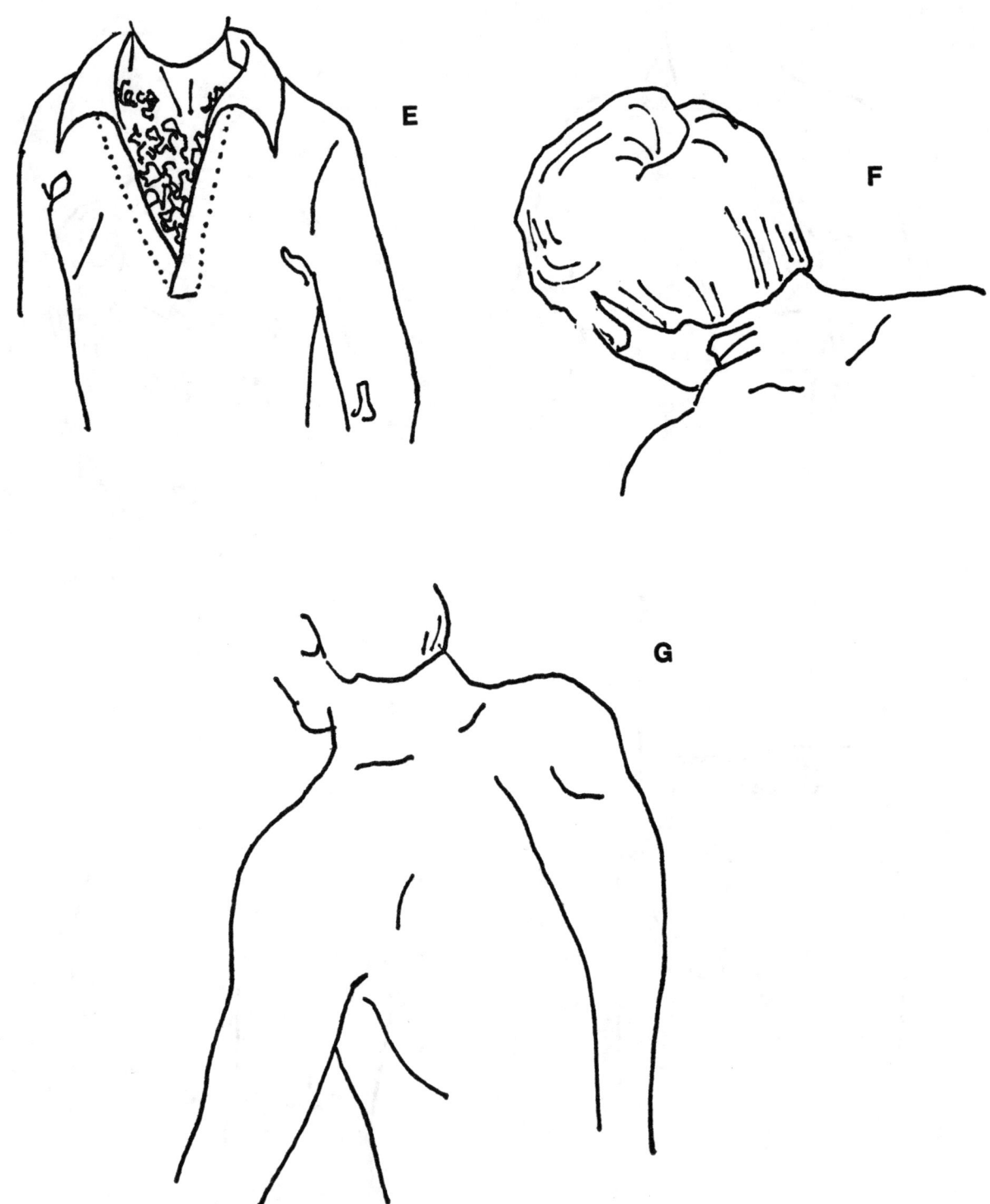

Scoring: It is important to recognize that this test involves generalization. Not everyone selecting a hairy chest, for example, falls within the same category. It also is an axiom that not every trait described under each selection will apply to everyone. With that in mind, let us take a look at the meanings of the selections you have made.

A. **Chest, No Hair.** Those ranking this first, value the gentle, creative, controlled, somewhat shy man. The women themselves tend to be slightly shy; they do not generally talk openly about sexual matters, they want to feel that they belong to their men and their men to them. Cleanliness and dress style are very much emphasized.

B. **Face.** Not surprisingly, those making this selection favor conversation and directness. Intellectual pursuits are important and, though these women may be sensual, they need conversation in order to be so. Generally, there is directness with all sexual matters and face-to-face contact always is vital. Control over emotion generally is strong.

C. **Lower Body.** Women making this selection have a deep, sensual interest in the male body. They have strong sexual needs and generally are very aware of this fact. They enjoy love-making and often like to get right to it with little preliminary conversation. These women generally are very confident in their own femininity and playful in their love-making.

D. **Buttocks.** This selection denotes a good deal of raw passion, and an active fantasy life. However, the tendency is to be indirect and experience fantasy in private. Sharing is difficult, and seldom is there much conversation about sexual activity. These women generally find a few other women to talk to about some portions of their fantasies, but they seldom share them with men. They are selectively aggressive, but only when they feel the man won't be shocked. They are, however, often inclined to experiment sexually with their men.

E. **Hairy Chest.** The major demand of this type of woman is that her man be rugged and aggressive. If a man isn't, he doesn't get a second chance. There also is a competing desire for a tender, affectionate and protective man. Intellectual pursuits are important, but they come only after it is clearly established that the man in question is rugged. There is a desire to be protected by her man and the woman prefers looking up to him.

F. **Hair.** Generally, this implies a heavy emphasis on appearances. The woman making this selection is likely to prefer men fastidious about their appearance, and to be highly involved with her own appearance. Man-woman interaction within this group involves a large amount of game-playing; action is slow to develop. These women generally seek an overabundance of support for their acceptance by someone. Insecurity is common and, although basically shy, these women act as if they were very confident. Often, they act as if they were center stage.

G. Shoulders, Back View. This is the selection that is least often made. It signals, in general, someone looking to identify with power. However, these women seldom interact deeply with their men. Things are on an indirect level, usually casual, and the woman generally is somewhat timid in her approach. She is likely to be an introvert and hold men, especially powerful appearing ones, in awe.

Conclusions: These are the personality types according to the selections made. No actual scoring categories exist, but one other observation should be made. Note the consistency, or lack of it, with the two selections. For example, E and F selections basically are incompatible. One is distinctly more sexual than the other. Such a selection suggests conflict over the two roles the lady would like to play. It is likely that the first would be the desired role and the second the role the lady feels she *must* play. The conflict between the two will cause a back-and-forth action, while two similar choices, e.g., B and F, will more likely reinforce one another. Behavior will be consistent in that case.

Now that you have a complete and accurate concept of that which you prefer, you are ready for step two. One of the most enjoyable aspects of this test is sharing what you have learned about yourself. This sharing should only be done with someone very special. It will tell your man how to dress to show off that aspect of himself that really turns you on. Perhaps you would like him to take special care with the appearance of his hair. Or perhaps you would like him to approach you in a somewhat different manner. Hopefully, this test will have given you some fun things to share.

A Man's Test Of Sexual Attraction
FOR MEN ONLY

Introduction: Most men agree that it is fun to look at women. After all, we have girl watcher's clubs, and even those who don't belong love the sport. The majority of men feel that they know what turns them on. Some men claim they like bosoms, others claim to prefer legs, others state an affinity for some other portion of the female anatomy.

The question is, do you really know? Those who claim to prefer bosoms may actually prefer legs. This author has known more than one man who has claimed to be turned on by curves, but yet has selected a rather flat woman. Is it possible that these men were not stating their real preferences? Are you aware that the type of woman you prefer tells something about your personality? Do you secretly yearn for a passive woman, while seeking assertive women? The following will test the accuracy of what you *think* you prefer. Test yourself and find out what *really* turns you on.

Instructions: Most men feel that they are more attracted to one part of the female anatomy. Here is a chance to test this theory and to see what your selections mean. Pick your first and second choices from the pictures that follow. Should you wish to rank all seven of the pictures, you may do so, but the first two count the most. After you have made your selections, read the scoring that follows the presentation of the pictures.

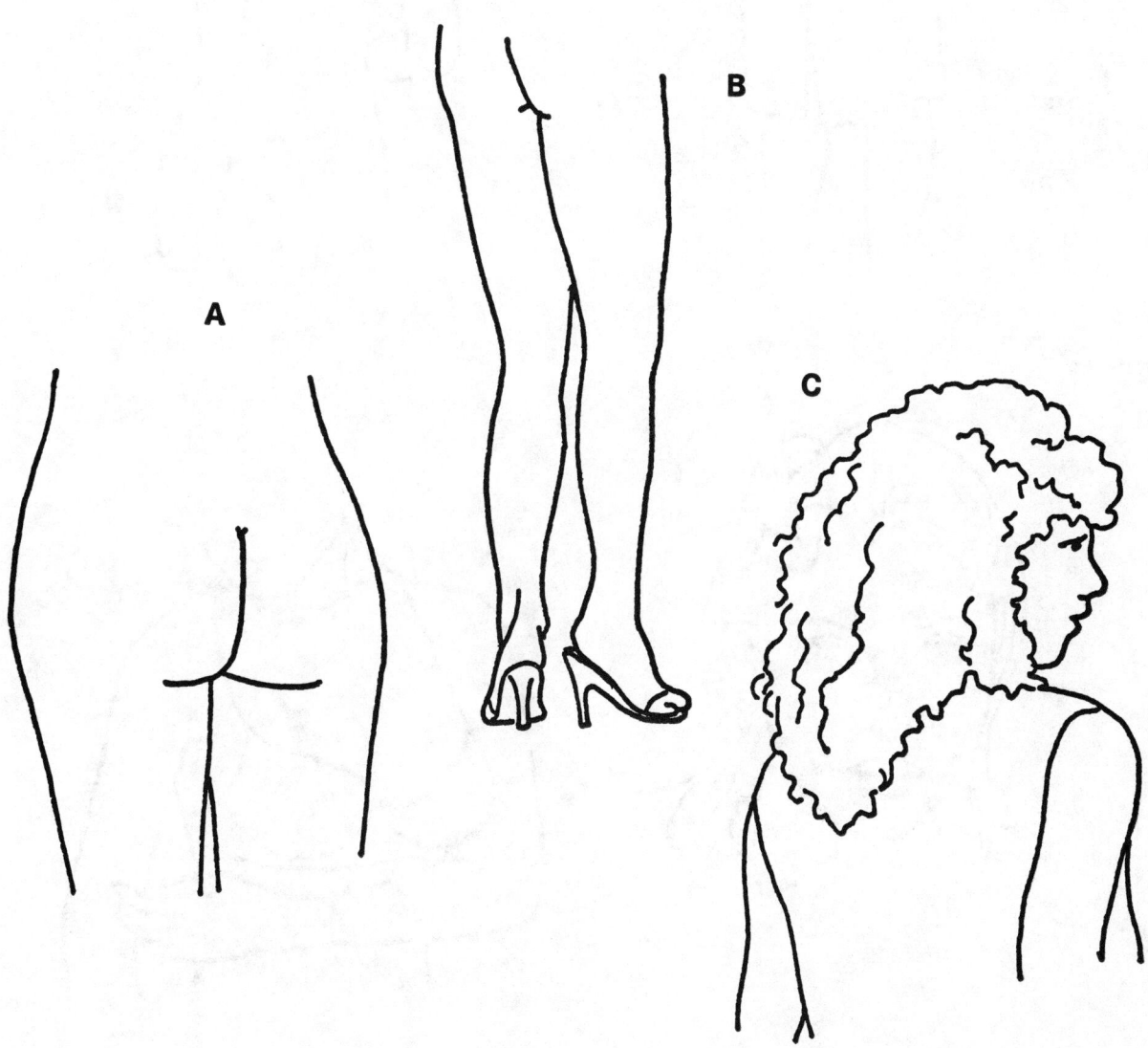

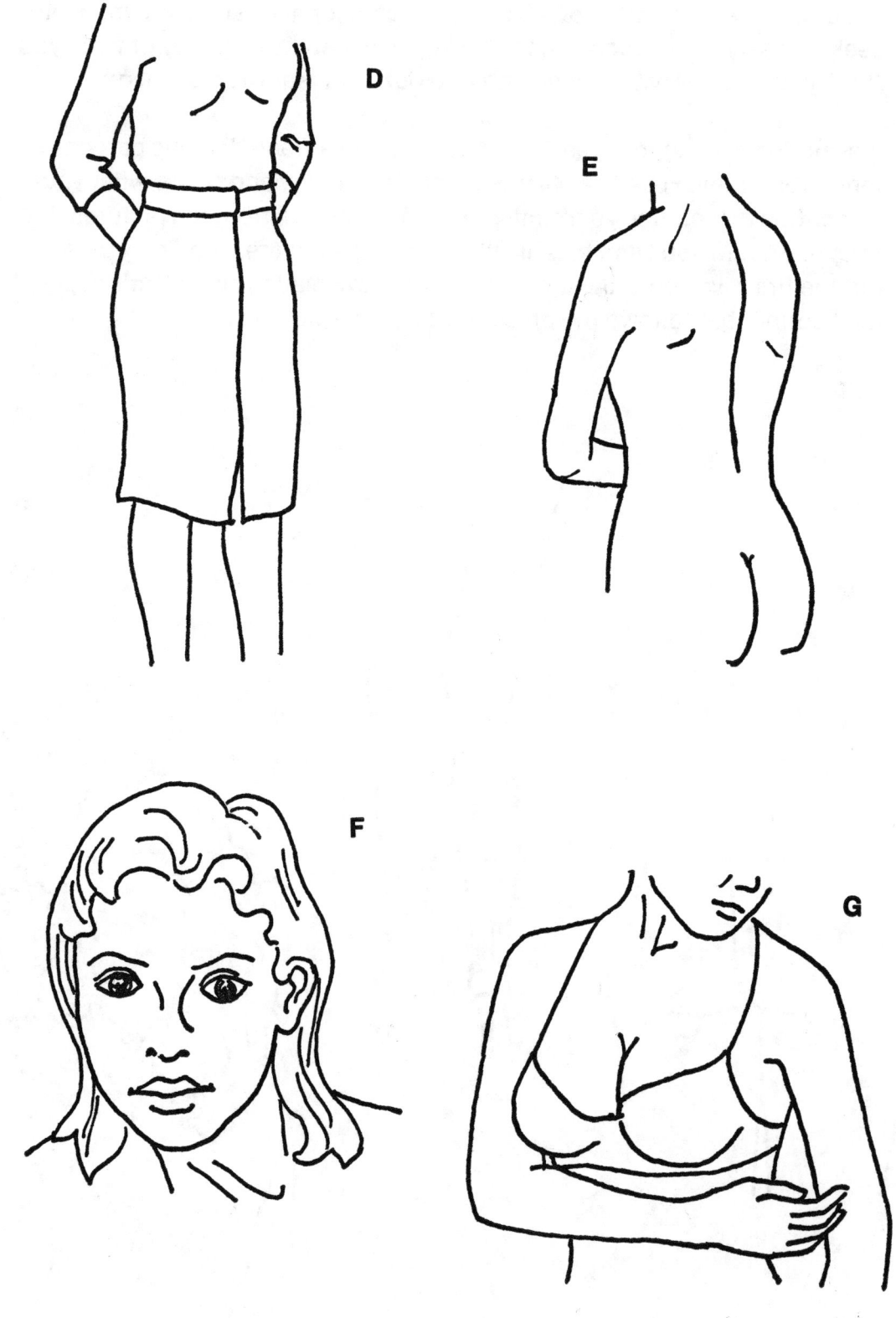

Scoring: It is important to recognize that this test involves generalization. Not everyone selecting a busty woman, for example, falls within the same category. It also is an axiom that not every trait described under each selection will apply to everyone. With that in mind, let us take a look at the meanings of the selections you have made.

    A. Buttocks. This was a popular choice of men in the "Gay 90's," but it no longer ranks No. 1. Men making this selection generally are rich in sexual fantasy but they find the gap between fantasy and reality difficult. They tend to be dreamers and they usually do not wish to share their fantasies. Guilt feelings are rather frequent and passivity with women is somewhat common.

    B. Legs. "Leg men" tend to drink less than the average man, but preferred size of legs also is important. Heavier legs are preferred by somewhat shy and submissive men, while thin legs most often are picked by extroverted men with exhibitionistic tendencies. Leg men have many quiet fantasies about women, but they share their fantasies only with close friends.

    C. Hair. Men making this selection prefer women who look soft and feminine. They enjoy affection and closeness, but they expect their women to follow more traditional lines of behavior. They do not like aggressive women and expect to be the dominant partner in the relationship. They are careful about their appearance and expect their women to be the same.

    D. Torso. Men who make this selection are rich in sexual fantasy and generally they are aware of their feelings. They need women who enjoy foreplay as well as love making. Making love is likely to be a full evening's activity and there is great anticipation for what lies ahead. Expectation is a large part of the game of love. Active women are preferred.

    E. Shoulders, Rear View. Very few men make this selection. Those who do, tend to be quiet, submissive, and often afraid to make a direct approach to their women. They may have sexual fantasies but they are not likely to share them with anyone. They frequently are guilt-ridden and often need dominant women.

    F. Face. This selection generally is made by men who enjoy conversation and equality in their sexual relationships. They enjoy talking to women, value good appearance, and share their fantasies with their women. They often are passionate men but their passion is tempered by solid intellectual controls.

    G. Bust. This selection generally is made by men who prefer large-breasted women. These men generally have dated extensively, are outgoing extroverts and active in sports. They are quick to become sexually aroused and free in talking about their fantasies. However, their dependency needs also are strong and these men must be wary that they are not easily manipulated by seductive women. Men who prefer small-breasted women tend to be more submissive, emotionally subdued, guilt-ridden and even mildly depressed.

Conclusions: These are the choices: one more step remains. Note whether your first and second choices clash (as would, for example, selections G and E). If so, then the first choice is more apt to be a conscious wish while the second choice is likely to represent a more hidden wish. The two choices either may reinforce one another or cause conflict. In the ideal case, the two choices may complement one another and thereby provide balance.

Men, now that you know what you like, shouldn't you share that knowledge with the special woman in your life? If you let her know that you really are a leg man, she can dress to accentuate her legs. If you like a woman's hair, she can spend particular attention to that detail. At the same time, having learned more about your personality, your woman will know better how to please you. Of course, you must do the same with her. Sounds like fun, doesn't it?

6. Preference Tests

    1. Individual Scale of Values
    2. Preferred Activities
    3. A Test of Sexual Attitudes

We all recognize that we prefer certain activities over others. Rare is the human being who likes everything to the same degree. Despite this obvious fact, many of us are unaware of many of our own preferences. The following tests help us find previously unknown preferences and, when shared with a loved one, we may find increased mutual understanding.

Individual Scale of Values

Introduction: Each person places great value upon something bigger than himself or herself. Whether we know it or not, we all have some guiding philosophy. Many of us have creative interests and yet we may be totally unaware of this fact. Or perhaps there is a hidden politician within us.

Many people come to a psychologist to find themselves. They feel as if they are drifting and not getting all they want out of life. Often, they want help in finding new interests and activities.

Sometimes, too, people with widely different values have difficulty in communicating. Creative people may take exception to the business world, and philosophically-minded individuals may clash with those who are very practical. It helps to know what one's bent is so that an allowance can be made when interacting with others of different orientation. This test should clearly help with all of these factors.

Directions: In each series there are names of famous people. Select that person whom you most admire, by noting the letter corresponding to that person's name. Scoring procedures are provided at the conclusion of the test.

1. Thomas Edison (B), Abraham Lincoln (D), Elvis Presley (F), General Patton (G), Harry S. Truman (A), Aristotle (H).

2. W. Clement Stone (I), Jimmy Carter (A), Benjamin Franklin (D), Pope Paul (E), Rembrandt (C), Ivan Pavlov (B).

3. Barbra Streisand (F), General Brown (G), Socrates (H), E. I. Dupont (I), F. Scott Fitzgerald (C), Dr. Jonas Salk (D).

4. Franklin D. Roosevelt (A), William Shakespeare (C), Ralph Nader (D), Billy Graham (E), General MacArthur (G), Plato (H).

5. Thomas Jefferson (H), Charles Darwin (B), Frank Lloyd Wright (C), Frank Sinatra (F), Bertrand Russell (H), J. P. Morgan (I).

6. Howard Hughes (I), Herbert Hoover (A), Helen Keller (D), General Moshe Dayan (G).

7. General Eisenhower (G), Martin Luther King (E), Bob Hope (F), John Locke (H), Henry Ford (I), Albert Einstein (B).

8. Dean Martin (F), Bishop Pike (E), Ernest Hemingway (C), George Gallup (D), J. P. Getty (I), Sigmund Freud (B).

9. Immanuel Kant (H), Leonardo Da Vinci (C), John F. Kennedy (A), General Bradley (G), Galileo (B), Saint Paul (E).

Scoring: The first step is to add up the total number of selections for each letter. Note that no letter can be selected more than six times.

The second step is to construct your value profile. This is done by drawing a vertical line that reflects the number of selections for each letter. The height of the line will reflect the value you place in each of the nine different areas of endeavor. Some persons may emphasize several areas, as for example, artistic and creative. Others may be rather even with all areas. Whatever the case, you should find it rather interesting to see what your profile of values reveals.

Conclusions: Now you have found those values that are most important to you. This knowledge should help you avoid foolish arguments with people who never will share your point of view. At the same time, you now may be able to bridge the gap with people who have similar values. Your new found knowledge also may help you select more satisfying reading material. You should have discovered a new you!

Profile of Values

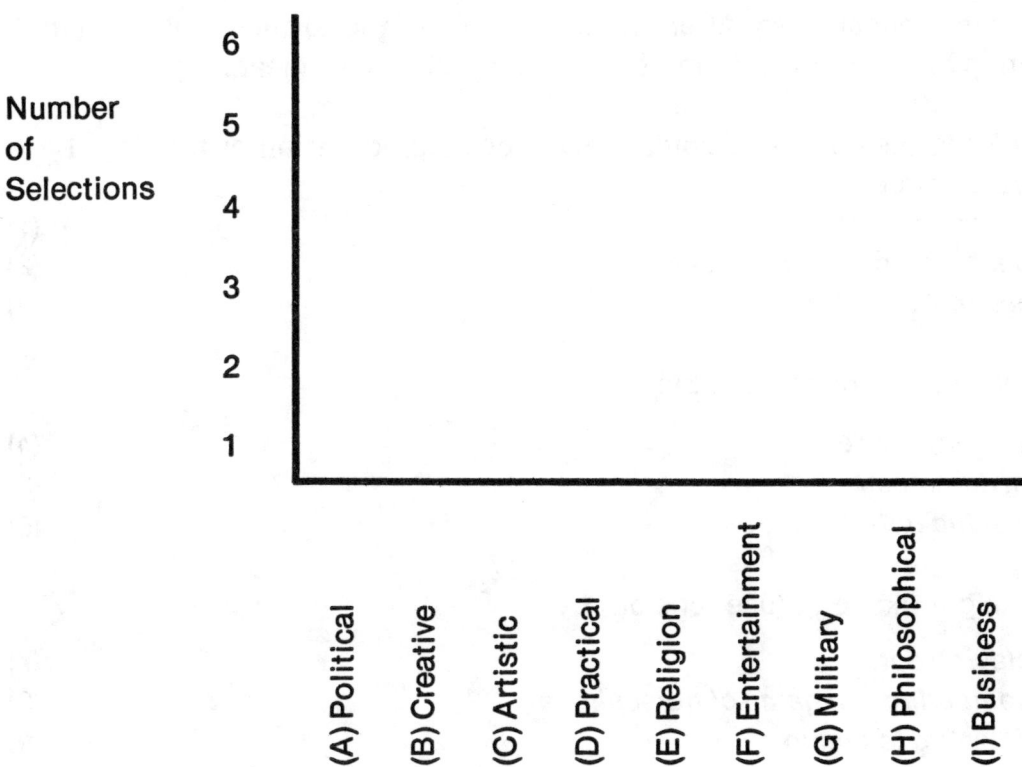

Preferred Activities Test

Introduction: Most people enjoy talking about themselves, and yet they do not really know themselves. To illustrate that point, note how often people describe themselves only in terms of their occupation. "I am a lawyer," says a new acquaintance. But isn't that person actually much more? Or, "I am a secretary." Again, you wonder what that really tells you.

The Preferred Activities Test helps uncover the hidden you—the "you" of likes and preferences. Would you secretly love to be a movie star, to have your handwriting analyzed, or to wage psychological warfare? Would you like to be more physically active, or more quietly intellectual? Do you wish or yearn to change your hobbies or even your job?

Even more importantly, what would a profile of your interests resemble? This test will show you that, and the results may surprise you. You may want more out of life than you heretofore have realized!

Directions: With each question you will be asked to state a preference. If you do not actually like any of the three choices, select the one you least dislike. You must, in each case, force yourself to check one of the three choices. Otherwise you will invalidate the test. Circle the number that indicates your choices. After you have answered the 40 questions, read the scoring directions to determine what your preferences mean.

1. If I had the chance to complete any desired education or training, I would choose:
a. to earn a Ph.D. (1)
b. become a plant supervisor (2)
c. become an actor (3)

2. I would select as a hobby:

a. growing flowers (4)
b. writing poetry (5)
c. playing golf (6)

3. I might like to reduce tension by:

a. playing darts (7)
b. competing at a game of horseshoes (8)
c. listening to music (9)

4. As a challenge, I would like:

a. planning a lecture (10)
*b. being editor of **Psychology Today** magazine* (11)
c. competing in a chess tournament (12)

5. Part of me yearns to:

a. be by myself to just think (13)
b. join a dance group (14)
c. swim one-half mile a day (15)

6. I always try to:

a. analyze my dreams (16)
b. win arguments (17)
c. solve puzzles (18)

7. When alone I enjoy:

a. watching TV (19)
b. analyzing my personality (20)
c. fishing (21)

8. I would like regularly to:

a. have an exercise program (22)
b. work crossword puzzles (23)
c. watch athletic games (24)

9. With someone special I would enjoy:

a. collecting sea shells (25)
b. going to parties (26)
c. horseback riding (27)

10. Of the following I least dislike:

a. balancing a check book (28)
b. arguing with a salesperson (29)
c. drinking alone at a bar (30)

11. My secret ambition is to:

a. wage psychological warfare (31)
b. do psychological research (32)
c. organize opposition to a government project (33)

12. I would most like to study:

a. mathematics (34)
b. psychology (35)
c. zoology (36)

13. If I had the time I would:

a. lie in a heated pool (37)
b. write a Congressman (38)
c. work in a home woodshop (39)

14. I wish I could improve:

a. the design of modern cars (40)
b. my vocabulary (41)
c. my physical condition (42)

15. It would be fun to:

a. lie in a hammock (43)
b. compose a song (44)
c. select prizes for my club (45)

16. I wish someone would teach me how to:

a. draw cartoons (46)
b. help protect wildlife (47)
c. direct a fund drive (48)

17. I wish I could:

a. just lie in the sun at a beach (49)
b. skin dive for shells (50)
c. have an intimate candlelight dinner (51)

18. One of my preferred sports would be:

a. playing doubles at tennis (52)
b. swimming in a race (53)
c. snowmobiling (54)

19. If I had the ability I would like to:

a. work on crafts (55)
b. conduct an advertising campaign (56)
c. act in a play (57)

20. Once I had a desire to:

a. have my handwriting analyzed (58)
b. paint a room in my home (59)
c. compete in a bocce tournament (60)

21. Of the three I would prefer:

a. wallpapering a bathroom	(61)
b. writing a report	(62)
c. winning at bridge	(63)

22. I would like to have been:

a. a cheer leader	(64)
b. a winner at public speaking	(65)
c. a more active person	(66)

23. I would prefer:

a. digging in a garden	(67)
b. a bridge club	(68)
c. winning a dance contest	(69)

24. It would be fun to:

a. walk through the woods in summer	(70)
b. be my club's social director	(71)
c. design clothing	(72)

25. I would love to:

a. explore caves	(73)
b. be honorary captain of my bowling team	(74)
c. decorate a float for a parade	(75)

26. I have always wanted to:

a. help reforest land	(76)
b. become head of a large company	(77)
c. learn a foreign language	(78)

27. A good leisure activity would be:

a. ice skating	(79)
b. analysis of my life goals	(80)
c. taking a self-scoring psychology test	(81)

28. I wish I could have become:

a. a comedian	(82)
b. a geologist	(83)
c. a psychologist	(84)

29. I secretly wish to:

a. enter a debating contest	(85)
b. practice my golf by myself	(86)
c. win a political campaign	(87)

30. I wouldn't mind the hard work if:

a. I could fight my way to the top	(88)
b. train a horse to do tricks	(89)
c. conduct a benefit	(90)

31. I wish someone would pay me to:

a. be able to spend time by myself	(91)
b. play handball	(92)
c. conduct a sales program	(93)

32. I would prefer:

a. playing baseball	(94)
b. decoding a message	(95)
c. playing solitaire	(96)

33. I wouldn't mind if I had to:

a. plan a speech	(97)
b. be a director of a college	(98)
c. help stock streams with fish	(99)

34. I would enjoy:

a. rehearsing a speech by myself	(100)
b. supervising other workers	(101)
c. working with two others on an art poster	(102)

35. I would willingly:

a. be elected president of my club	(103)
b. reflect on the day's events	(104)
c. sketch with charcoal	(105)

36. I would prefer:

a. writing a book	(106)
b. studying soil erosion	(107)
c. sculpture in clay	(108)

37. It would be more fun to:

a. go bowling	(109)
b. read a book	(110)
c. convince others that my point is correct	(111)

38. I would be most willing to:

a. conduct, with others, a business meeting	(112)
b. go skeet shooting	(113)
c. take color photographs	(114)

39. I would most like to:

a. be elected to Congress	(115)
b. win a legal battle	(116)
c. counsel young people	(117)

40. A preferred activity would be:

a. becoming a salesperson	(118)
b. establishing a personnel testing program	(119)
c. solving a murder mystery	(120)

Scoring: When you have completed the test, you will have made 40 selections. Your answers will indicate which of the 12 areas of interest you emphasize. Check the numbers of your selections against the following.

Answer Number

Sedentary—I   9, 10, 19, 24, 28, 37, 43, 49, 62, 110

Social—II   14, 26, 51, 52, 57, 64, 68, 82, 90, 112

Solitary—III   13, 30, 80, 86, 89, 91, 96, 97, 100, 104

Competitive—IV   8, 12, 31, 53, 60, 63, 65, 69, 87, 88

Active—V   15, 22, 39, 42, 50, 55, 59, 61, 66, 67

Sporting—VI   6, 7, 21, 27, 54, 79, 92, 94, 109, 113

Psychological—VII   11, 16, 20, 32, 35, 58, 81, 84, 117, 119

Persuasive—VIII   17, 29, 33, 38, 56, 85, 93, 111, 116, 118

Intellectual—IX   1, 18, 23, 34, 41, 44, 78, 95, 106, 120

Artistic—X   3, 5, 40, 46, 72, 75, 102, 105, 108, 114

Leadership—XI   2, 45, 48, 71, 74, 77, 98, 101, 103, 115

Nature—XII   4, 25, 36, 47, 70, 73, 76, 83, 99, 107

Finally, you might wish to construct an interest profile.

Preferred Activities

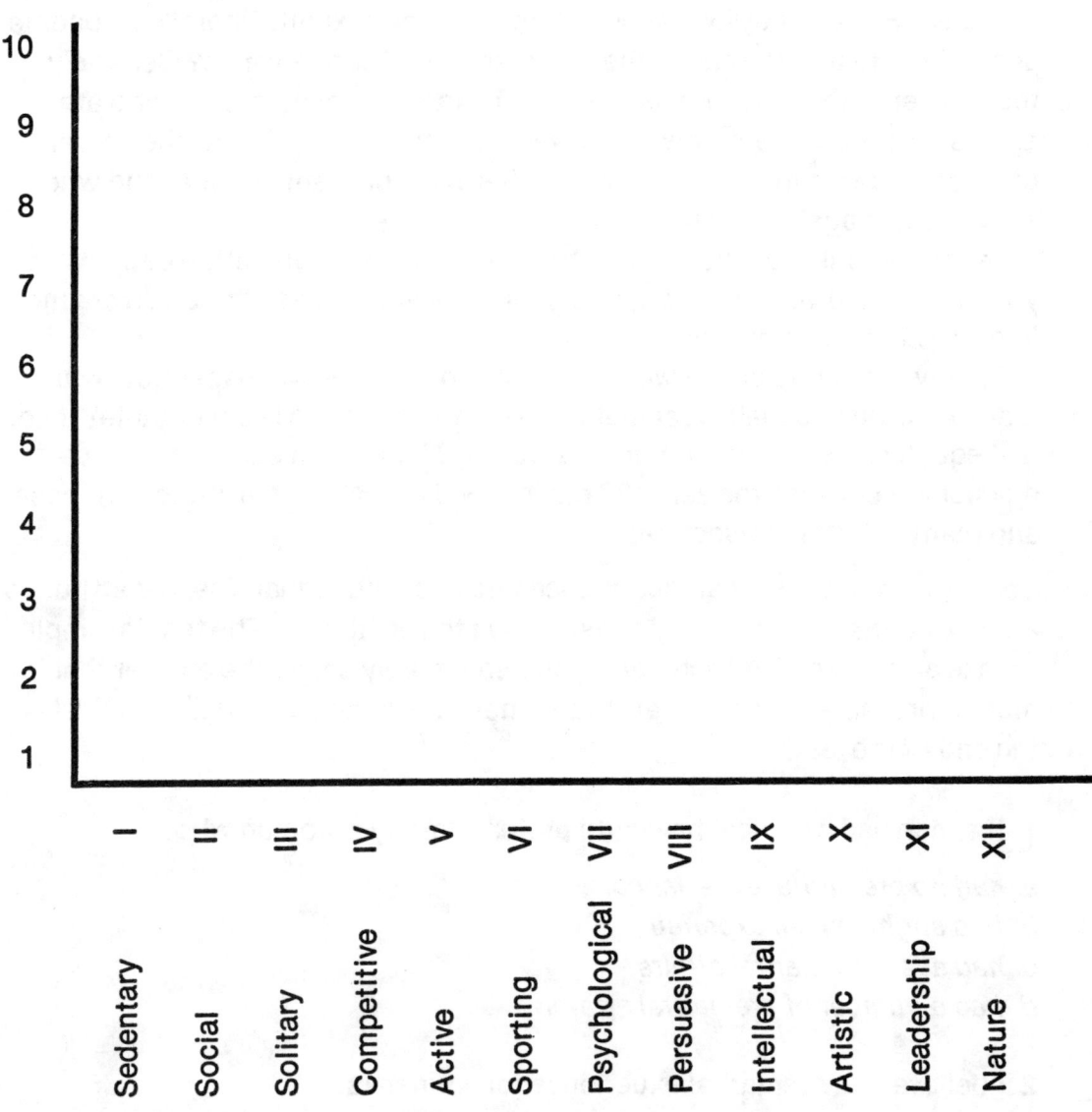

Conclusion: You may be surprised by the results of your test. Some important questions may have been answered. What new hobbies might you now pursue in light of your test scores? Should you perhaps consider a new job? Should you seek out new friends with similar preferences in order to have more to share? Should you try a wider variety of activities in the hopes of fulfilling some of your new-found preferences? At least, you now can identify yourself by more than your occupation. You may just have discovered what an interesting person you are!

A Test of Sexual Attitudes

Introduction: This test gives the reader an opportunity to take a good look at his or her thinking. These days, many people claim to be sexually liberated. But are they? What does it mean to be sexually liberal? Do people generally find that they are either all liberal or all conservative? Generally, the answer to that question is, "no." For example, many people who are against abortion may otherwise be very liberal. It is important, therefore, to identify your pattern of attitudes. Where do you want change, and where are you most against change?

Secondly, this test should help breach some communication gaps. When you understand your position, you should be able to see where you are most likely to both share and clash with others.

Finally, selecting an answer forces you to put down on paper how you really feel. Do you really feel that premarital experience is acceptable? If so, is it equally acceptable for men and women? How open should be sexual discussion between the sexes? This test will reflect your attitudes on these and many other vital questions.

Scoring: This test is designed to measure each individual's sexual attitudes along a continuum from very conservative to very liberal. The test is simple to take and score. For each item, you need merely select the answer that is most representative of your attitude. Then check the scoring and analysis at the end of the test.

1. If a man had a choice, he would prefer to marry a woman who:

a. had no premarital experience.
b. had slight sexual experience.
c. had a few premarital affairs.
d. had a number of premarital affairs.

2. I believe that premarital experience for women is:

a. very damaging.
b. does not produce any change.
c. is helpful for future marital success.
d. is highly desirable.

3. Knowledge about sex is:

a. not desirable for women.
b. not important for women.
c. very important for women.
d. exceedingly important for women.

4. A woman's sex drive generally is:

a. not as strong as a man's.
b. unknown as far as intensity.
c. nearly as strong as a man's.
d. at least as strong as a man's.

5. Knowledge about sex generally is:

a. not necessary for a man.
b. slightly desirable for a man.
c. important for a man.
d. extremely important for a man.

6. A woman should:

a. tell her fiance about her sexual experiences.
b. admit only what she has to.
c. not tell her fiance anything of her past.
d. share with her fiance her experiences.

7. A man should:

a. tell his fiance about his sexual experiences.
b. admit only what he has to.
c. not discuss his premarital experience.
d. share with his fiance his experiences.

8. Curiosity about sex:

a. exists predominantly for men.
b. exists slightly more for men.
c. is about equal for both men and women.
d. is equal for both sexes.

9. Direct requests for sexual activity:

a. are the option of men.
b. seldom are allowable for women.
c. are equally acceptable for both sexes.
d. are needed equally from both sexes.

10. Sexual desires:

a. should not be discussed openly.
b. can be alluded to.
c. should be discussed openly.
d. must be discussed openly.

11. Sexual activity is acceptable:

a. only during married life.
b. when there is a formal commitment.
c. when two people share a mutual desire.
d. when two responsible people feel they want it.

12. Sex for fun:

a. is not acceptable.
b. seldom is allowable.
c. is only excusable in marriage.
d. should be a part of all sexual relationships.

13. Sexual experimentation and exploration:

a. is not ever acceptable.
b. rarely is acceptable.
c. is healthy.
d. should be a part of all sexual relationships.

14. Men are attracted by nudity and that is:

a. unhealthy.
b. normal but very dangerous.
c. normal.
d. desirable.

15. Women's attraction to nude males:

a. is most rare.
b. happens and may not be harmful.
c. is very desirable and healthy.
d. is as healthy and desirable as a man's attraction to nude women.

16. Movies which are X-rated:

a. should be banned for all.
b. should be more carefully censored.
c. are bad but need not be restricted.
d. may be stimulating to a husband and wife.

17. Seductive clothes:

a. should be avoided by women.
b. are dangerous.
c. may be acceptable under a few circumstances.
d. help both men and women feel good.

18. If a person feels sexually unfulfilled he or she should:

a. not mention it to anyone.
b. read books to find what is wrong.
c. discuss it openly with his or her lover.
d. discuss it and explore to find that which feels fulfilling.

19. **Playgirl** magazine:

a. should not be sold.
b. is dangerous.
c. may not, after all, be too damaging.
d. is good because it allows women the same opportunities that men have.

20. Male masturbation:

a. is very destructive.
b. never should be discussed.
c. is acceptable.
d. may serve as a healthy outlet.

21. Female masturbation:

a. is very disruptive for emotional growth.
b. should not be discussed.
c. may not be harmful.
d. may provide useful benefits.

22. Male adultery:

a. is a terrible thing.
b. seldom happens but is overly talked about.
c. happens frequently.
d. may take place for a wide variety of reasons.

23. Female adultery:

a. is a terrible thing.
b. seldom happens but is more often talked about.
c. probably happens more and more frequently.
d. may well involve numerous different motives.

24. If adultery takes place:

a. a crime has been committed.
b. a marriage is over.
c. it will put a strain on any marriage.
d. the couple should try to understand what caused the affair.

25. Oral sex:

a. is not a desirable act.
b. never should be discussed in mixed company.
c. is no big deal.
d. is fine if both partners enjoy it.

26. Sex guides:

a. never should be written because sex already is overly emphasized.
b. are not really needed.
c. are fine for a few who are troubled.
d. may help many couples put variety into their love-making.

27. Petting and foreplay:

a. are necessary sometimes before intercourse.
b. are helpful for intercourse.
c. are fun.
d. should not have a clear ending since all of love-making should be play.

28. Abortion:

a. should be illegal.
b. never is morally acceptable.
c. is acceptable only in rape cases.
d. should be a personal issue.

29. A woman's sexual fantasies:

a. should not be discussed openly.
b. are greatly overplayed.
c. are not well understood.
d. may well be as active as a man's.

30. A woman's sexual fantasies:

a. should not be a part of her love-making.
b. may not harm her love-making.
c. may well enhance her love-making.
d. probably are essential to the most passionate of love-making.

31. The sexual liberation of women is:

a. damaging to the relationships between the sexes.
b. probably inevitable.
c. desirable.
d. only fair since society has long allowed greater freedom to men.

32. The so-called "double code of morality" or different rules for men and women, is:

a. a very workable moral code.
b. acceptable though it has some weaknesses.
c. is not fair to women.
d. is not fair to either sex since it makes it difficult for men and women to relate.

33. Sexual gadgets are:

a. something that never should be manufactured.
b. disgusting.
c. not needed.
d. fine for those who enjoy them.

34. Birth control information:

a. is immoral.
b. should not be publicized.
c. sometimes is beneficial.
d. should be provided for everyone who wishes it.

35. Sexual behavior should:

a. be governed by the society.
b. be controlled by religious leaders.
c. have established guidelines set by our religious groups.
d. be an individual choice as long as consenting adults are involved.

36. If you meet someone with a sexual code very different from your own you should:

a. avoid that person.
b. tolerate that person.
c. not be disturbed by it.
d. accept this behavior as right for him or her.

37. If you learned that your spouse had a homosexual experience in his or her youth you would:

a. naturally be terribly hurt.
b. try to be understanding.
c. not be concerned.
d. recognize it as not at all abnormal.

38. If someone makes a pass at your mate, you would:

a. hit the offending person.
b. be angry at your mate.
c. let the situation determine your reaction.
d. have faith that your mate can handle it.

39. Frank, open sexual talk:

a. is too prevalent in our society.
b. should not take place in mixed company.
c. is not always destructive.
d. should take place between the sexes.

40. A sexual climax is:

a. vital for a man's well being.
b. more likely for men than for women.
c. desirable for both sexes.
d. equally needed for both men and women in a meaningful relationship.

Scoring: Upon completion of this test, there should be 40 selected answers. Simply total the number of times you have selected answer A, answer B, answer C, and answer D.

Answer A indicates the most ultra-conservative individual, the one who usually does not want change or open discussion. Answer B shows a less conservative person, one who may at times allow openness. Answer C individuals are moderately liberal and they allow greater change and openness. The answer D person is the ultra-liberal who wants changes and freedom.

Few persons will select all of one type of answer. A profile such as that provided will permit you to note the role which each level of the liberal-conservative spectrum plays in your sexual attitudes. A simple line graph will quickly present your profile and, if you choose, you may compare notes with your mate or lover.

Conclusion: Now that you see where you stand on some important issues, maybe you can understand how you interact with others. Do you clash, for example, with people who resist change or with people who want change? Should you share your test answers with your lover? Might this not open up some important areas of communication? If properly used, this test may help you examine some of your attitudes, prejudices and biases. It also may help bring you closer to a loved one. At least, you may both be able to gain respect for the views of one another. Who knows, at some point you may even be able to examine the reasons behind your attitudes.

Profile of Sexual Attitudes.

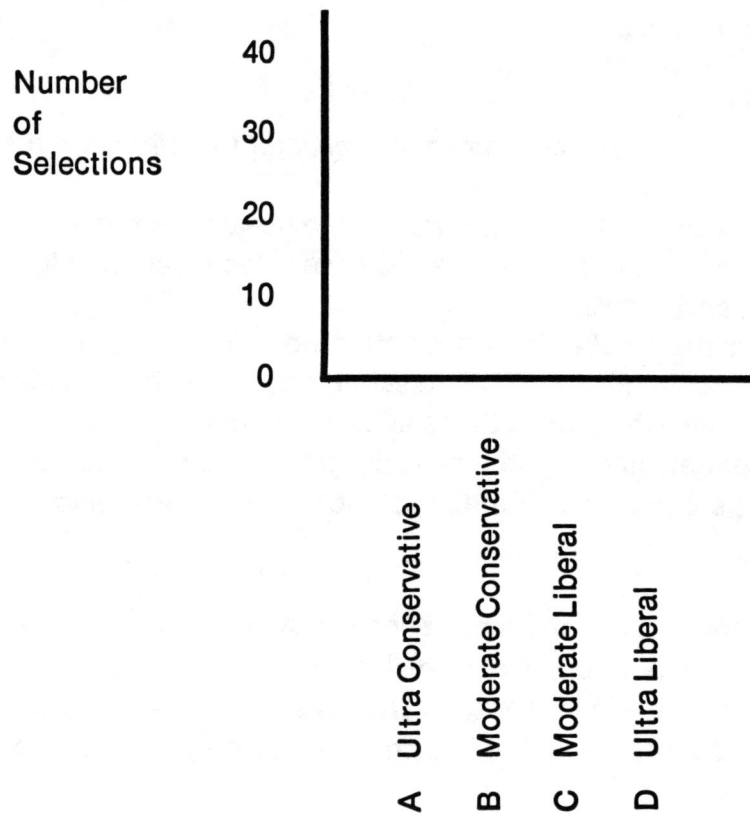

7. Memory Tests

1. Memory For Digits
2. Memory for Objects
3. Memory for Designs

Have you ever impressed someone by remembering some fact about that person? Do you remember names of people after initial introductions? Do you easily recall birthdates and anniversaries of important people in your life? Can you remember the way to the homes of your friends after one visit? Do you know your social security number?

In these days of numbering everything and everyone, memory skills are very important. The three memory tests that follow measure your ability to remember numbers, objects and abstract designs. The Memory For Digits Test can be taken auditorily or visually. At any rate, these tests will show how you compare with others and will locate your strengths and weaknesses. Should you wish to improve your memory, there are many books available on the subject. There is much evidence that memory can be improved dramatically.

Try to relax and enjoy the challenge: your performance will improve.

A Memory For Digits

Introduction: The following test measures the ability to concentrate on a task, learn quickly, and then demonstrate good memory. This test measures what is called short-term memory—unlike, for example, a test of vocabulary, which measures permanent knowledge.

Instructions: Using a small card, cover all of the digits below those on which you are working. Read each digit at the pace of one per second. Look away and write the digits from memory. Discontinue when you have failed both sets of a series. Then proceed the same way with the digits in reverse, i.e., read forward and write in reverse.

A second method of administering the test would be to have someone else read the digits at about one per second. You then are measuring short-term auditory memory.

Digits	Digits in Reverse
1. 6-7-1	3-9
9-4-3	8-4
2. 7-5-8-2	7-4-2
2-9-3-1	9-1-8
3. 6-9-1-7-2	6-2-8-5
7-2-4-8-5	3-5-4-9
4. 1-5-3-2-8-4	9-3-7-4-8
2-7-4-9-1-5	3-7-5-9-2
5. 2-9-4-6-3-7-1	3-8-1-6-4-9
1-5-2-9-8-6-3	1-8-3-6-5-9
6. 3-8-5-2-1-7-4-6	4-6-1-9-2-7-3
7-9-3-1-5-2-4-6	2-9-4-6-1-8-5

Scoring: Add total correct forward and reverse.

Number Correct	Rating
15	fantastic
14	very superior
13	very good
12	high average
11	average
10	low average
9	far below average
8 & under	very weak memory

Memory For Objects

Instructions: This test of visual memory is simple to take. Look at the objects for twelve seconds, then look away and list the objects you have seen.

Scoring:

Number Correct	Rating
15-17	excellent
13-14	very good
11-12	average
9-10	below average
8 & under	poor

Note: A clue toward a better memory is to group related items. For example, this test becomes easier when you form three groups—men's and women's clothing and things that you eat, drink or that otherwise relate to the mouth.

Memory For Abstract Designs

By their very nature, abstract designs are difficult to remember. Being strictly a product of someone's imagination, they bear no similarity to anything familiar or natural. This test will measure your ability to remember a picture of something which is totally unfamiliar to you.

Instructions: Look at each design for five seconds. Then look away and draw the designs from memory.

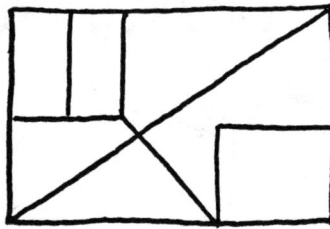 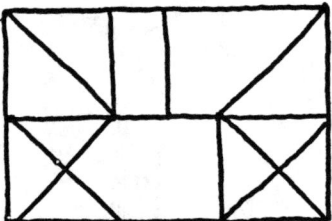

Scoring: Count the number of correctly drawn lines and then score as follows:

Number correctly drawn	Rating
23-25	far superior
19-22	superior
16-18	well above average
14-15	average
12-13	below average
11 & under	poor